Jackson   12/24/90

County

Library

System

HEADQUARTERS:

413 W. Main

Medford, Oregon   97501

GOD
WITH US

GOD
WITH US

*The Miracle
of Christmas*

John F. MacArthur, Jr.

Zondervan Books
Zondervan Publishing House
Grand Rapids, Michigan

GOD WITH US: THE MIRACLE OF CHRISTMAS
Copyright © 1989 by John F. MacArthur, Jr.

Zondervan Books
are published by Zondervan Publishing House
1415 Lake Drive, S.E.
Grand Rapids, MI 49506

Library of Congress Cataloging-in-Publication Data

MacArthur, John, 1939–
    God with us : the miracle of Christmas / by John F. MacArthur, Jr.
      p.   cm.
    ISBN 0-310-28690-5
    1. Christmas. 2. Jesus Christ—Nativity. 3. Incarnation.
4. Virgin birth. I. Title.
BV45.M32   1989
232.92'1—dc20   89–34273
                                                                    CIP

All Scripture quotations in this book, except those noted otherwise, are from the New American Standard Bible, © 1960, 1962, 1963, 1968, 1971, 1972, 1973, 1975, and 1977 by The Lockman Foundation, and are used by permission.

The illustrations in this book are for decorative purposes and do not presume to be biblically or historically accurate. The illustrations on pages 2, 11, 21, 36, 76, 112, 117, 128, and 131 were reproduced with the kind permission of the Bettmann Archive, whose research proved invaluable to this project.

Printed in the United States of America

89 90 91 92 93 94 95 / DH / 10 9 8 7 6 5 4 3 2 1

CONTENTS

INTRODUCTION

We're in danger of losing Christmas. It may now be the biggest and most popular of all our holidays, but Christmas is in jeopardy just the same. A subtle but sure erosion is eating away the season's true significance.

You may wonder what I'm talking about. After all, someone will ask, isn't Christmas the one time each year when people of every persuasion—religious or not—celebrate the highest of human values? We talk and sing, don't we, of peace on earth, goodwill toward men? We extol the spirit of peace, brotherhood, charity, and kindness. We put everything else on hold while we gather with our families to give one another gifts and commemorate the holiday. And when all is said and done, don't those things capture the essence of Christmas?

Not quite. Those certainly are good, wholesome virtues. They are, however, mere vestiges of the real meaning of Christmas.

What Christmas is *really* about is the birth of Jesus—Immanuel, God with us, the promised Messiah—who came to save His people from their sins (Matthew 1:21). If it's not immediately clear to you why that truth transcends all others, this book is for you. We will look closely at some of the key elements of the biblical account of Christmas. We'll see exactly why the birth of a baby two thousand years ago should be important to us today. I hope you'll come away with a new and deeper understanding of Christmas.

I offer this book hopefully as an antidote to two prevailing philosophies that are stealing Christmas. One is *an effort to mythologize* the Christmas story, and the other is *a tendency to secularize* it.

When I speak of the effort to mythologize Christmas, I'm referring to the way the world has reduced it to little more than an elaborate fable. Over the years, singers and storytellers have embellished the legend so much that most people don't know which details are biblical and which are fabricated. Tradition has turned the unnumbered visitors from the East into three kings and has even given them names. Popular songs place animals in the stable and personify them like characters out of Aesop. We usually imagine the manger scene with snow, singing angels, many worshipers, and a little drummer boy. None of that is found in the biblical account.

Did you know, for example, that the magi—wise men—did not visit Jesus the night of His birth? Scripture tells us they found Him in a house (Matthew 2:11). This might have happened weeks, even months, after Jesus was born. These men probably were not kings, and there is no indication that there were only three of them. The facts about them have been lost in the mythology that has overgrown the biblical account.

The other hazard, coming from a different direction, is the growing tendency to secularize Christmas. I'm not referring entirely to the ubiquitous Santas, reindeer, and talking snowmen that dominate our Christmas decorations, although that is part of it. What concerns me most is that the spiritual values of Christmas are giving way to crass consumerism. Christmas has become the ultimate holiday for committed hedonists. Drunken parties, self-indulgence, madcap spending, and obscene gluttony all characterize the way much of the world celebrates Christmas.

The trends are not hard to document. Visit your local shopping mall during the week before Christmas, and you'll witness graphic evidence of how Christmas is rapidly slipping away from us. Notice how stores advertise their merchandise—and notice *what* they advertise. Listen to the shoppers talk. Stop by a card store and look at the greeting cards. Try to imagine that you are someone who has never heard of Christ or Christmas. What message would you get from what you see?

More important, what does our Lord think of all this? That question continually weighs on me. Can we rationalize all this self-indulgent excess by calling it a celebration of His birth—He whose cradle was only an animal's feeding trough?

I read a haunting newspaper story several years ago about a wealthy Boston family who had a christening party for their new baby. They invited all their friends and relatives to their magnificent home to celebrate the birth of their precious infant. A half hour into the party, when it was time to bring the baby out for everyone to see, the mother made a tragic discovery. The large bed where she had left the baby asleep was piled high with the coats of the guests. The baby was lying dead underneath the mound, suffocated by the carelessly discarded wraps.

That pathetic scene perfectly illustrates what the world has done to Christmas. Lost is the realization that Christmas is first of all a celebration of the birth of the Savior. He is all but forgotten, cruelly and thoughtlessly smothered in the haste and commotion.

Please understand, I'm not suggesting that our Christmas celebrations should be solemn, somber, grim religious observances utterly devoid of cheer. On the contrary, Christmas should be a time of real joy and gladness, as opposed to the manufactured sentiment and wild revelry that characterizes the way the world observes Christmas.

That true joy comes from a realization of what Christmas is really all about and from knowing the One whose birth we celebrate.

We can't know Him if we don't understand He is real. The story of His birth is no allegory. We dare not romanticize it or settle for a fanciful legend that renders the whole story meaningless. Mary and Joseph were real people. Their dilemma on finding no room at the inn surely was as frightening for them as it would be for you or me. The manger in which Mary laid Jesus must have reeked of animal smells. So did the shepherds, in all probability. That first Christmas was anything but the picturesque scene we often envision.

But that makes it all the more wondrous. That baby in the manger is God.

That's the heart and soul of the Christmas message. There weren't many worshipers around the original manger—only a handful of shepherds. But one day, every knee will bow before Him, and every tongue will confess He is Lord (Philippians 2:9–11). Those who doubt Him, those who are His enemies, those who merely ignore Him—all will one day bow too, even if it be in judgment.

How much better to honor Him now with the worship He deserves! *That's* what Christmas ought to suggest.

My prayer is that as you read this book you'll come to see the truth of Christmas and all its richness in a way you've never seen it before. May this be the most wonderful Christmas you have ever celebrated.

A Christmas Prophecy

The Lord Himself will give you a sign: Behold, a virgin will be with child and bear a son, and she will call His name Immanuel. Isaiah 7:14

A child will be born to us, a son will be given to us; and the government will rest on His shoulders; and His name will be called Wonderful Counselor, Mighty God, Eternal Father, Prince of Peace. Isaiah 9:6

All this took place that what was spoken by the Lord through the prophet might be fulfilled, saying, "Behold, the virgin shall be with child, and shall bear a Son, and they shall call His name Immanuel," which translated means, "God with us."
Matthew 1:22–23

A little girl came home from Sunday school triumphantly waving a paper. "Mommy!" she said. "My teacher says I drew the most unusual Christmas picture she has ever seen!"

The mother studied the picture for a moment and concluded it was indeed a very peculiar Christmas picture. "This is wonderfully drawn, but why have you made all these people riding on the back of an airplane?" the mother gently asked.

"It's the flight into Egypt," the little girl said, with a

hint of disappointment that the picture's meaning was not immediately obvious.

"Oh," the mother said cautiously. "Well, who is this mean-looking man at the front?"

"That's Pontius, the Pilot," the girl said, now visibly impatient.

"I see. And here you have Mary and Joseph and the baby," the mother volunteered. Studying the picture silently for a moment, she summoned the courage to ask, "But who is this fat man sitting behind Mary?"

The little girl sighed. "Can't you tell? That's Round John Virgin!"

We laugh, but the sad truth is that little girl's mixed-up perspective of Christmas is not really much more muddled than the notions the average person carries around. Christmas has become an elaborate fabrication, and our celebrations reflect that. The cast of characters we bring out at Christmas is no less bizarre than the ensemble that little girl put on her airplane. Our Christmases are the product of an odd mixture of pagan ideas, superstition, fanciful legends, and plain ignorance. The real message of Christmas is all but lost in the chaos.

Let's try to sort it out.

Back to the Source

The place to begin is in God's Word—the Bible. Here we find not only the source of the original account of Christmas, but also God's own commentary on it.

The Christmas story in the Bible begins earlier than you might expect—several hundred years earlier. One Old Testament prophecy after another promised a coming Savior—the Messiah, the Anointed One—who would redeem the people of God. The centerpiece of all the Christmas prophecies, Isaiah 9:6, was written by Isaiah nearly six

Key Old Testament Prophecies Fulfilled at Christmas

A star and a scepter came out of Israel	Numbers 24:17; Matthew 2:1–2
Messiah was born of a virgin and called "Immanuel," meaning "God with us," (Jesus Christ was God in human form)	Isaiah 7:14; Matthew 1:18–25
He was born in Bethlehem	Micah 5:2; Matthew 2:1–6; Luke 2:1–7
Messiah descended from Jesse (David's father), and the Spirit of the Lord rested upon Him	Isaiah 11:1–3; Matthew 1:1–17; 3:16
The Lord raised up a great Prophet	Deuteronomy 18:15–19; John 7:40

hundred years before Jesus' birth. Writing under divine inspiration, Isaiah was able to see across the centuries and give us an amazingly accurate picture of the Savior's birth. He promised it would be a miraculous event, unlike any the world had ever known. The details Isaiah gave were fulfilled too precisely for the connection to be dismissed as chance.

Isaiah foretold, for example, that Jesus would be born to a virgin—a woman who had never been sexually intimate with any man. We will have much more to say in chapter 3 about this critical truth. For now we simply note that it was one of the most startling details of Isaiah's prophecy. Isaiah 7:14 says, "The Lord Himself will give you a sign: Behold, a virgin will be with child and bear a son, and she will call His name Immanuel." That virgin's name was Mary.

The name *Immanuel,* however, is the key to this verse—and the heart of the Christmas story. It is a Hebrew name that means literally, "God with us." It is a promise of incarnate deity, a prophecy that God Himself would appear as a human infant, Immanuel, "God with us." This baby who was to be born would be God Himself in human form.

If we could condense all the truths of Christmas into only three words, these would be the words: "God with us." We tend to focus our attention at Christmas on the *infancy* of Christ. The greater truth of the holiday is His *deity.* More astonishing than a baby in the manger is the truth that this promised baby is the omnipotent Creator of the heavens and the earth!

The Promise of a King

To the Jewish nation, Isaiah's prophecy was news of a coming King. The child who would be born, Isaiah said, would shoulder the government (9:6). To the unsuspecting world, the prophecy promised a Savior, God incarnate, whose coming would dramatically and forever alter human history.

Isaiah 9:6 is surely the most familiar of all the Old Testament prophecies about the birth of Christ. Handel included it as one of the great choruses of his *Messiah* oratorio. Chances are you either sing it or hear it several times every Christmas season.

Consider the rich truth in this one short verse. Observe, for example, the unusual names given to this extraordinary Son: "Wonderful Counselor, Mighty God, Eternal Father, Prince of Peace." Those are remarkable titles for a baby, aren't they? This was no ordinary child, but one whose coming had been long awaited. Three phrases at the beginning of the verse hint at who He really is.

Son of man. "A child will be born unto us" is a statement about His humanity. He began life like any other human—as an infant. Isaiah doesn't say any more here, but we know from the New Testament that throughout His life Christ experienced every temptation common to humanity, but He never sinned (Hebrews 4:15). Ultimately He would die as all men die, yet not for any sin of His own but bearing all humanity's sin and guilt. As a man, He felt everything we feel, hurt like we hurt, wept like we weep, and in His death, He even felt the weight of sin.

Son of God. Notice the second phrase, "a son will be given to us." Not "born"; "*given*." The terminology speaks of the Savior's preexistent deity. Again, we know the full truth of what Isaiah only suggests: that He existed before His birth. Already God, the second Person of the Trinity, He was given to us to be our Savior. "Although He existed in the form of God, [He] did not regard equality with God a thing to be grasped, but emptied Himself, taking the form of a bond-servant . . . being made in the likeness of men" (Philippians 2:6–7). He came as the Son of God—God in a human body—to conquer sin and death forever. He is the perfect Son of God, the promise of the ages, the Holy One of Israel, the desire of nations, the light in darkness, the only hope for our lost world.

King of kings. "The government will rest on His shoulders" looks beyond that first Christmas to a time still in the prophetic future when Christ shall reign over a literal, earthly, geopolitical kingdom that encompasses all the kingdoms and governments of the world (see Zechariah 14:9; Daniel 2:44). In that day, the government of the whole world will rest on His shoulders, and He will reign as sovereign over a worldwide kingdom of righteousness and peace.

In the meantime, His government operates in secret. His kingdom and sovereign rule are manifest within those who trust Him and obey Him as their Lord. Although the King is not presently reigning in visible form, He rules in the hearts of His people (see Luke 17:20–21). That rule, like the future worldwide kingdom, is marked by righteousness and peace. In fact, all the characteristics of the future earthly kingdom are reflected to some degree in this present, invisible kingdom.

A Different Kind of Kingdom

What are those characteristics? What distinguishes Messiah's dominion from worldly governments? The names Isaiah uses in his Christmas prophecy signal four unique features that make Messiah's kingdom—in both its present and future manifestations—different from any other power on earth.

No Confusion—He Is a Wonderful Counselor. First, Messiah's kingdom has the answer to the world's confusion. The King in charge is a Wonderful Counselor. The King James Version separates "Wonderful" and "Counselor" with a comma, but they seem to go better together and appear that way in most modern versions.

During His incarnation, Christ demonstrated His wisdom as a counselor. Study the New Testament descriptions of Jesus' encounters with people who came to Him for counsel. In a marvelous way, He always knew what to say, when to reach out to a seeking heart, and when to rebuke an impetuous soul. The testimony of those who heard Him was, "Never did a man speak the way this man speaks" (John 7:46).

Christ is the source of all truth. He said, "I am the way, and the truth, and the life" (John 14:6). It is He to whom we must ultimately turn to make sense of life's confusion.

Unfortunately, most people turn everywhere *else* for counsel. They go to psychologists, psychiatrists, analysts, philosophers, religious quacks, astrologers, and other human advisers. But the most critical truth of all—the only really life-changing truth—is the truth that is found in Jesus Christ. He is the ultimate and only answer to all of life's confusion.

Wouldn't you like to have a counselor who knows everything? Jesus is that counselor. He knows all about you; He knows all the needs of your heart; He knows how to answer those needs. And He always gives wise counsel to those who will hear and obey Him.

No Chaos—He Is the Mighty God. Second, His kingdom is singularly free from chaos. The King is the Mighty God. He is the powerful One who in creation brought order out of chaos.

Scripture says, "God is not a God of confusion, but of peace" (1 Corinthians 14:33), meaning chaos is antithetical to who He is. He is a God of order with the power to create it.

Christ the King loves to step into a life of chaos and not only provide wonderful counsel, but also display His divine power by bringing order to the chaos. In other words, He not only tells His subjects what to do as a Wonderful Counselor, but He can also energize them to do it—because He is the Mighty God.

Human counsel goes only so far; it stops short at the point of power—that is, a human counselor has no ability to empower someone to do right. Put that together with the reality that this world's wisdom is so foolish (1 Corinthians 3:19), and you can see why human counsel usually only leaves worse chaos in its wake.

But in Jesus we have a sovereign Master who is not dependent on the wisdom of this world. He is God, and because He is God, He can forgive sin, defeat Satan, liberate people from the power of evil, redeem them, answer their prayers, restore their broken souls, and reign over a rebuilt life, bringing order to our chaos.

No Complexity—He Is the Father of Eternity. We tend to cringe at the word *government,* picturing an administrative labyrinth with a complex mass of red tape. Our Messiah's kingdom is not like that. He requires no bureaucracy; He needs no support staff; He shoulders His government by Himself. He can do it because He is the Eternal Father, or as Isaiah 9:6 is literally translated, "the Father of Eternity."

Once again, this phrase is a reference to the biblical truth that Christ is Creator of heaven and earth. In Hebrews 1:10–12, God the Father, speaking to Christ the Son, says, "Thou, Lord, in the beginning didst lay the foundation of the earth, and the heavens are the works of Thy hands; they will perish, but Thou remainest; and they all will become old as a garment, and as a mantle Thou wilt roll them up; as a garment they will also be changed. But Thou art the same, and Thy years will not come to an end." In other words, according to God the Father's own testimony, the Son— Jesus—was the Person of the Godhead who created time out of eternity and fashioned the universe from nothing.

Nothing is too difficult for the Creator and Sustainer of everything. Infinity and all its intricacies are nothing to Him who is the Alpha and Omega, the First and Last, the

Beginning and the End—the Father of eternity. He declares the end from the beginning (Isaiah 46:10). That is, from the very start, He declares how everything will turn out. What a comfort to know that He is in complete and sovereign control, He sees the end of everything, and He guarantees that all things will work together for the ultimate good of all His kingdom's subjects (Romans 8:28). That promise alone takes away a lot of chaos, doesn't it?

The world is getting more and more complex. And human governments seem to exist primarily to make it that way! We build bureaucracies, thinking that's the only way to deal with the complexities of life—and consequently life only grows more perplexing.

But Messiah's government is simple and uncomplicated.

Isaiah, prophesying about the kingdom, wrote of the highway of holiness: "the unclean shall not pass over it, but it shall be for those; the wayfaring men, though fools, shall not err therein" (Isaiah 35:8 KJV). His way is so free from complexity that even fools cannot lose their way.

No Conflicts—He Is the Prince of Peace. Finally, in Messiah's kingdom there are no conflicts, because He is the Prince of Peace.

He offers *peace from God* (Romans 1:7) to all who are the recipients of His grace. He makes *peace with God* (Romans 5:1) for those who surrender to Him in faith. And He brings *the peace of God* (Philippians 4:7) to those who walk with Him.

As we hear so often at Christmas, the beginning of His earthly life was heralded by angels who announced *peace on earth* (Luke 2:14).

There never really has been peace on earth, in the sense we think of it. Wars and rumors of wars have characterized the entire two millennia since that first Christmas, and all the time before it.

That announcement of peace on earth was a two-pronged proclamation. First, it declared the arrival of the only One who ultimately can bring lasting peace on earth (which He will do when He returns to bring about the final establishment of His earthly kingdom).

But more important, it was a proclamation that God's peace is available to men and women. Read the words of Luke 2:14 carefully: "Glory to God in the highest, and on earth peace among men *with whom He is pleased.*"

Who are those with whom He is pleased? The ones who have yielded their lives to the authority of His government: "The Lord taketh pleasure in those who fear him, in those who hope in his mercy" (Psalm 147:11 KJV).

Why should we fear Him and hope in His mercy? Because we are sinners in need of forgiveness (Romans 3:23). We must first recognize our sinfulness if we are to place our lives under His government. But the good news is that Christ gave His own sinless, guiltless life on our behalf, to die for our sins and save us from God's wrath (Romans 5:6–9). We can do nothing to earn His favor, but He promises salvation if we will turn from our sins and embrace Him by faith (Ephesians 2:8–9; Romans 6:23).

So when the angels proclaimed peace on earth, they were speaking primarily of a very personal, individual application of God's peace that grows out of a firsthand knowledge of the Prince of Peace.

Isaiah 9:7 goes on to say, "There will be no end to the increase of His government or of peace, On the throne of David and over his kingdom, to establish it and to uphold it with justice and righteousness from then on and forevermore. The zeal of the Lord of hosts will accomplish this."

In other words, His perfect government and perfect peace will keep expanding, getting better and better. That reminds me of the chorus of a familiar hymn, "Like a River Glorious." It speaks of peace that is "perfect, yet it groweth fuller ever day. Perfect, yet it floweth deeper all the way."

How can anything perfect get better? That's one of the mysteries of Messiah's government. It just gets better and better, and the perfect peace gets deeper and deeper.

And so we have the message of Christmas in prophetic form. It is the good news of God's answer to all the confusion, chaos, complexities, and conflicts of life. It is the gift of One who is a newborn infant and yet was the Father of all eternity. He is but an innocent child, yet He is a wise counselor and mighty King. He is God with us. If you find those realities hard to fathom, you've glimpsed the truth of Christmas.

Think of it: His shoulders are broad enough for the government of an eternal kingdom. And still His compassion is such that He offers His peace and His kingdom to people like you and me, though we have rebelled against His righteousness. He is eternally sovereign, yet He chose to become a baby, so that He might live in our world—as Immanuel, God with us.

Unto *us* a child is born. Who is "us"? Everyone? No. In context, Isaiah is speaking of those who believe—who rejoice in God (Isaiah 9:3). There is no Savior, no hope, no peace, no eternal life, no mighty power, and no wise counsel for those who do not know Jesus Christ.

But those who embrace Him by faith are ushered into His kingdom. Their lives are transformed by His power. He becomes their Counselor. And it keeps getting better and better!

May the government of your life be on His shoulders.

Christians and Christmas

Christmas as a holiday was not observed until well after the biblical era. The early church of the New Testament celebrated Jesus' resurrection, but not His birth. In fact, Christmas was not given any kind of official recognition by the church until the mid-fifth century.

Partly because so many Christmas customs seem to have their roots in paganism, Christians have often been resistant to some of the rituals of the holiday. The Puritans in early America rejected Christmas celebrations altogether. They deliberately worked on December 25 to show their disdain. A law passed in England in 1644 reflected a similar Puritan influence; the law made Christmas Day an official working day. For a time in England it was literally illegal to cook plum pudding or mince pie for the holidays.

Christians today are generally not opposed to celebrating Christmas. The holiday itself is nothing, and observing it is not a question of right or wrong. As the Paul wrote, "One man regards one day above another, another regards every day alike. Let each man be fully convinced in his own mind. He who observes the day, observes it for the Lord, and he who eats, does so for the Lord, for he gives thanks to God; and he who eats not, for the Lord he does not eat, and gives thanks to God" (Romans 14:5–6). Every day—including Christmas— is a celebration for us who know and love Him.

How we observe Christmas is the central issue. Do we observe it for the Lord's sake or for our own sinful self-gratification? Do we even think about why and how we celebrate it? That is the heart of the matter. Christmas is an opportunity for us to exalt Jesus Christ. We ought to take advantage of it.

Knots on the Family Tree

Jesus' ancestry may surprise you. His genealogy includes some names you might be shocked to find in the royal line of the King of Kings. Four women in particular stand out. Not only is it unusual to find women listed in a Hebrew genealogy, but these women are particularly noteworthy because they contrast so dramatically with the absolute purity and righteousness of God's Anointed One. All of them were outcasts, yet they made it into Jesus' family album. They are a strong assurance of God's grace to sinners like us.

One of our family's Christmas traditions has always been the reading of the Christmas story from the gospels. We've done it every year as long as I can remember. When I was a child, my father read the account from either Matthew or Luke while we sat at his feet. Now I do the reading, and my own children gather to listen.

A few years ago while studying through Matthew I pondered the question of why our family readings of Matthew 1 always start in the middle of the chapter. Matthew begins his account of Christ's birth with a broad genealogy, but we had never made it a part of our Christmas reading.

Skipping the genealogy in a family reading is understandable, especially when you've got small children who are easily bored. I'm the first to admit that the genealogies in Scripture don't make the most stimulating public readings.

But realizing that we were skipping this passage in our Christmas celebration piqued my curiosity, and I began to study Matthew 1:1–17 in earnest. It was spellbinding. Virtually every name in the list reveals some lesson about God's grace. Together they show clearly how important God's grace was from generation to generation as He nurtured and protected the lineage He had chosen to give birth to the Messiah.

A Chronicle of God's Grace

The genealogies are included in Scripture for that very reason. Not only do they trace the royal line of Israel, but they also outline God's dealings with His people. They reveal how God's sovereign hand has ordered human events to fulfill His own purposes despite tremendous obstacles. Mankind's worst sin, rebellion, and treachery have utterly failed to thwart the grace of God.

The lineage of Judah's kings went back to David. God's promise was that David's offspring would bring forth the One who would deliver Israel and reign as King. In 2 Samuel 7:16, speaking through the prophet Nathan, God promised David, "Your house and your kingdom shall endure before Me forever; your throne shall be established forever."

What this meant was that any claimant to the throne of Israel had to demonstrate genealogically that he descended from David and was in the line of royalty. Scripture records the infallible and authoritative record of that lineage.

The genealogies had other practical uses in Old Testament Israel. They were often essential for the conducting of important business. Laws governing the buying and selling of property, for instance, were designed to keep internal boundaries intact. Land could not be bought and sold across tribal lines. Therefore a person's genealogy was required simply to validate the sale of property.

The entire priesthood also depended on genealogies. All Israel's priests had to be descendants of Levi. After the Babylonian captivity, Ezra used the genealogies to determine which priests had a legitimate claim to office. Those who couldn't prove their heritage could not serve as priests.

For all those reasons, the genealogies were carefully recorded and guarded. The most important ones were preserved in Scripture. This practice went on for centuries, through the time of Jesus' birth.

In fact, when the New Testament begins, we find Joseph and Mary going down to be registered according to their own ancestry in Bethlehem, their ancestral home (Luke 2:3–4). The nation still identified people genealogically.

A Look at the Apparent "Contradictions"

Two Genealogies. The two final genealogies in Scripture both trace the lineage of Jesus (Matthew 1:1–17; Luke 3:23–38). Some see these two genealogies as contradictory. A close look shows they are not. Matthew starts with Abraham and follows the line through David to Jesus via Joseph's family. Luke starts with Jesus and outlines the genealogy of Mary's family back through David and all the way back to Adam.

Note that Matthew doesn't refer to Joseph as Joseph the father of Jesus, but as "the husband of Mary, by whom was born Jesus" (Matthew 1:16). Scripture is clear that Joseph was not the father of Jesus; God was.

Because Jesus had no human father, He couldn't be a descendent of David except through His mother. Still, the legal right to rule always came through the father's side, and this was true even in Jesus' case, because He was legally Joseph's eldest son. Thus we have two necessary genealogies. Luke shows that through Mary Jesus was literally a blood descendant of David. Matthew proves that through His adopted father Joseph, Jesus was legally in the royal line. In every way possible, He had the right to rule.

Two Prophecies. In fact, Jesus' ancestry was an elegant solution to one of the most troubling dilemmas of Old Testament Messianic prophecy. God had cursed the royal line. Jeremiah 22:30 records God's judgment on Jeconiah, also known as Coniah, or Jehoiachin: "Thus says the Lord, 'Write this man down childless, a man who will not prosper in his days; for no man of his descendants will prosper sitting on the throne of David or ruling again in Judah.'"*

God meant business. Jeconiah was indeed the last king in the Davidic line. He was succeeded on the throne of David not by his son, but by his uncle, Zedekiah (2 Kings 24:17). Zedekiah's reign marked the end of Judah as a kingdom. And so Jeremiah's prophecy was literally fulfilled. Not one of Jeconiah's sons or any of their descendants ever again returned to the throne. It was a sad end to the Davidic dynasty.

Jeremiah's prophecy seems at first to be a glaring contradiction to the Messianic promise. Messiah was to be in the royal line of David, yet that line was effectively ended with Jeconiah. How could these two equally inspired, infallible prophecies both be fulfilled? Messiah *had* to come from the royal lineage of David and thus be a descendant of Jeconiah. But how could He ever rule as king without violating the prophecy that no descendant of Jeconiah would ever reign?

The fact is, if Jesus had been the *literal* son of Joseph,

---

*This does not mean Jeconiah would actually *be* childless, but rather that the effects of the curse would nullify the birthright. The lineage of kings would end; his children would not be his heirs. His right to rule, as well as all the other privileges of the royal birthright, were permanently taken from him and his descendants. The royal line was in essence terminated, as if Jeconiah had been childless.

born of his seed, He never could lay claim to the throne of David. He would be under the curse. And yet because He was still the *legal* son of Joseph, He inherited the right to rule, for He was not under the curse that had been passed down to everyone born in the royal line since the days of Jeconiah.

A Tale of Four Outcast Women

Looking closely at the royal lineage as Matthew records it, we note a striking anomaly. Four women are named in this genealogy. The typical Hebrew genealogy excluded women. To find four women's names in a single, brief genealogy is remarkable.* Even more extraordinary is that none of these four women epitomizes the kind of person we would expect to find in the royal heritage of the King of kings. All of them were outcasts.

Tamar. The first is Tamar: "To Judah were born Perez and Zerah by Tamar" (Matthew 1:3). What kind of woman was Tamar? Her story, if you want to read it in its entirety, is in Genesis 38. It is a sordid tale of incest, prostitution, and deception.

Judah had chosen Tamar as a wife for his firstborn son, Er. Er was evil. We don't know what he did, but God struck him dead for it (Genesis 38:7). Er's brother Onan then became Tamar's husband, as the law at that time required. When he spitefully refused to father children by Tamar, God struck him dead too (v. 10).

Frustrated at being childless, and unwilling to wait on the Lord's timing for the right husband, Tamar concocted an evil scheme to become pregnant. She dressed up as a

---

*Matthew obviously did not intend this to be a comprehensive genealogy. He was merely showing the line of descent, not naming each generation, and so in some cases he purposely omitted whole generations of minor names.

prostitute, put a veil over her face, and waited by the road until Judah, her own father-in-law, came along. Not realizing who she was, Judah committed a sinful act of fornication with his own son's widow (v. 18). Twin sons were conceived through that shameful act of harlotry and incest. Their names were Perez and Zerah. Perez, who was born first, carried on the Messianic line.

That is a shocking tale! Did you realize a woman like Tamar was part of Jesus' ancestry? Don't bother looking for her redeeming virtues. Almost nothing more is said about Tamar in the Old Testament account. Scripture records no happy ending to her life. She's really just a footnote in the early history of the Jewish nation, but she stands as a classic illustration of the frailty and utter sinfulness of humanity.

Perhaps that is the very reason Matthew mentions Tamar so prominently in this genealogy. If God would continue the Messianic line through Tamar's offspring—the product of incest, harlotry, fornication, and deception—He must surely be a God of grace.

Rahab. The next woman Matthew mentions may be more familiar to you. She's referred to in Scripture as "Rahab the harlot" (Joshua 6:17, 25; Hebrews 11:31; James 2:25). The name *Rahab* itself means "pride," "insolence," "savagery."

Rahab was a Canaanite, a mortal enemy of God's people. When we first encounter her in the biblical account, she is nothing more than an idolatrous, outcast Gentile woman, a professional prostitute. Her most memorable act was telling a lie.

Joshua 2 records that part of her story. After forty years of wandering in the wilderness, the Israelites were finally preparing to enter the Promised Land. Joshua had sent spies to scout out the city of Jericho. They happened upon Rahab, who hid them in her home. When city officials came looking for the men, Rahab lied to protect them. Knowing that the Israelites would destroy Jericho and everyone in it, she bargained with the spies to save her family. They agreed to spare her and them if she hung a cord of scarlet thread from her window to let the attacking Israelites know which house was hers.

She did, and the Israelites spared Rahab and her family. Rahab abandoned the gods of the Canaanites for Jehovah. She became not only a convert to the true God, but also a part of the Messianic line. She was the great, great grandmother of David.

Ruth. Rahab was the mother of Boaz. Matthew's genealogy continues: "To Boaz was born Obed by Ruth" (v. 5). Here, just one generation later, is another Gentile woman in the Messianic line. Unlike Rahab or Tamar, Ruth was not a prostitute or fornicator. But like them she was a Gentile.

Ruth was a Moabite. The entire Moabite race was a product of incest. The incident is chronicled in Genesis 19:30–38. Lot was living in a cave with his two daughters after the cities of Sodom and Gomorrah had been decimated. The daughters were fearful that there would be no one to marry them and carry on the family. So the eldest of the two suggested a scheme to get their father drunk and have sex with him.

Lot, Scripture says, had no idea what was happening, but his daughters on two successive nights each took a turn at getting him drunk and luring him into incestuous fornication. Both girls became pregnant. Scripture says, "Thus both the daughters of Lot were with child by their father. And the first-born bore a son, and called his name Moab; he is the father of the Moabites to this day. And as for the younger, she also bore a son, and called his name Ben-ammi; he is the father of the sons of Ammon to this day" (Genesis 19:36–38).

Thus Ruth was from a tribe of people who were the product of incest. Their very existence was repugnant to the Jewish people. Deuteronomy 23:3 is one of the laws that governed worship in Israel: "No Ammonite or Moabite shall enter the assembly of the Lord; none of their descendants, even to the tenth generation, shall ever enter the assembly of the Lord."

Yet Ruth became the wife of Boaz. Like Rahab, she converted to the truth and found grace in the eyes of God. Her great grandson was David.

Bathsheba. There's more. Matthew 1:6 mentions a fourth woman without naming her: "To David was born Solomon by her who had been the wife of Uriah." Who was it that had been the wife of Uriah? Bathsheba. Her story is not pretty either.

Bathsheba, according to 2 Samuel 11, was on a rooftop bathing herself when David saw her and lusted after her. He had his servants bring her to him, and he had a secret sexual relationship with her. It wasn't secret very long. Their union produced a child.

When David learned that Bathsheba was pregnant, he tried to cover their sin by bringing Uriah, Bathsheba's husband, back from the front lines of battle, where he was loyally serving David. David assumed that Uriah would have normal relations with his wife. Then no one would ever know that the baby was not Uriah's.

But David's attempts to cover his sin with Bathsheba failed. Uriah was more a man of integrity than he. As a matter of principle he refused to spend the night with his wife while his men were sleeping in tents on the battlefield. David wouldn't give up. He even got Uriah drunk, but Uriah would not compromise.

When David realized he could not cover his sin by making Uriah think he was responsible for Bathsheba's pregnancy, he sent a note to his commanding generals ordering them to put Uriah on the front line and fall back in the thick of the battle, leaving Uriah to be killed. In effect, he murdered Uriah.

Worse, he took Bathsheba to be his own wife. The child conceived by their fornication died shortly after birth. David ultimately was confronted with his sin and repented. Bathsheba conceived again and bore a son, Solomon. Solomon became the next link in the Messianic line. And thus Bathsheba, though guilty of an act of sinful adultery, also became part of the line that would culminate in the birth of Jesus.

What a genealogy Matthew gives us! It's almost as if he is nominating people for a Hall of Shame. Here are two harlots, one cursed Moabite, and an adulteress. These are the only four women mentioned in the entire genealogy, and every one of them was an outcast. Add Jeconiah and all the evil kings of Judah that preceded him, and it begins to seem like Jesus' royal genealogy was filled with sinners.

But that's just the point. Matthew, writing his gospel for an expressly Jewish audience, must have realized that by deliberately emphasizing these four women, he was confronting the self-righteous arrogance of the pharisaic tradition. The reality that the Messianic line was populated with Gentiles, fornicators, adulteresses, liars, cursed kings, and other sinners was something most of Matthew's readers would have preferred to ignore. That's the kind of truth men's writings frequently gloss over, but the Bible—because it is the inerrant Word of God—consistently refuses to obscure what is truly important.

Why? Because the people in the Messianic genealogy are not on display; God's grace is. Bathsheba and Rahab, for example, are memorable not because of their sin, but because of God's mercy in forgiving them. Rahab is mentioned two other times in the New Testament, in Hebrews 11:31 and James 2:25. Both times she is cited as an example of genuine faith. Whatever her background as a Gentile and prostitute, she will spend eternity in heaven, not because of anything she did, but because the God she turned to is a God of grace and mercy.

Jesus Christ is the friend of sinners (Luke 7:34). He Himself said, "I did not come to call the righteous, but sinners" (Matthew 9:13). He came to live among sinful men. He experienced what we experience. He was tempted in every way we are tempted, yet He was completely without sin (Hebrews 4:15). Nevertheless, He took on Himself the punishment for our sins. That's the grace of God.

How devastating this genealogy is when we see it for what God intended it to be! It strikes a blow in the face of legalism, self-righteousness, and human religion. It underscores the truth that Jesus identified with sinners. It puts a holy spotlight on God's grace.

You may skip the genealogy when you read the Christmas story aloud. But don't overlook its message of grace, which after all is the heart of the Christmas story: God in His mercy doing for sinners what they cannot do for themselves—mending broken lives and restoring shattered hopes. That's why He came—to save His people from their sins (Matthew 1:21).

Here's the best part: the same grace that was evident in the genealogy is active today, and the same Jesus is saving His people from their sins. No sin, no matter how heinous, puts sinners beyond His reach. "He is able to save them to the uttermost that come unto God by him, seeing he ever liveth to make intercession for them" (Hebrews 7:25 KJV).

Where Did Christmas Trees Come From?

Christmas trees seem to have their origins in the ancient celebrations of Saturnalia. The Romans decorated their temples with greenery and candles. Roman soldiers conquering the British Isles found Druids who worshiped mistletoe and Saxons who used holly and ivy in religious ceremonies. All those things found their way into Christmas customs.

Interestingly, however, the first person to have lighted a Christmas tree may have been Martin Luther, father of the Reformation. He introduced the practice of putting candles on trees to celebrate Christmas, citing Isaiah 60:13 as biblical authority for the practice: "The glory of Lebanon will come to you, the juniper, the box tree, and the cypress together, to beautify the place of My sanctuary; and I shall make the place of My feet glorious."

Is the Virgin Birth Really Essential?

No other fact in the Christmas story is more important than the virgin birth. The virgin birth must have happened exactly the way Scripture says. Otherwise, Christmas has no point at all. If Jesus is simply the illegitimate child of Mary's infidelity, or even if He is the child of Joseph's natural marital union with Mary, He is not God. If He is not God, His claims are lies. If His claims are lies, His salvation is a hoax. And if His salvation is a hoax, we are all doomed.

A lost football is a sad Christmas memory, but it's one of the vivid recollections of my adolescence. Athletics had become one of my youthful joys. I especially loved football, and for Christmas I wanted a real leather football of my own.

My dad was a pastor, and we lived on a lean budget. A leather football was a major purchase. I'm certain my parents had to sacrifice to get me the football I wanted.

Somehow they got it. The football was my favorite gift that Christmas, and I could hardly wait to get outside to play with it. I remember spending several happy hours that Christmas morning tossing it around with my dad and some of the kids in the neighborhood.

I don't remember who had the football when my mother called us in for lunch, but I assumed someone would bring it in. No one did. When I looked for it after lunch, the

football was gone. We had left it on the lawn, and someone had taken it.

It was a bitter lesson, but I never made a similar mistake again. I learned from that experience that it is important to guard carefully what we consider precious.

That is true in the spiritual realm as well. If we don't guard what is precious, the enemy, Satan, will try to steal it from us. His typical strategy is to try to make some small but foundational element of a great truth appear insignificant, then ridicule or call into question that issue. If he can get people to doubt or deny the smallest foundational truth, he can eventually destroy the entire superstructure. That's why issues like the inerrancy of Scripture are so important. If the Bible is the Word of God, it must be truth unmixed with error. Each detail—including the historical, geographic, and scientific ones—*must* be accurate. If we doubt even one point of biblical truth, we open the door to every other variety of denial and unbelief. History verifies the inevitability of this pattern.

The virgin birth is such an issue. Some people see it as a nonessential point, or treat it as mythology. It is neither. Although the church has not always been careful to guard this precious truth, it is the foundation of everything Christmas stands for.

Attacks on the Virgin Birth

A few years ago I read an interview with the pastor of one of our nation's largest churches. Asked specifically what he believed about the virgin birth, he said, "I could not in print or in public deny or affirm the virgin birth of Christ. When I have something I can't comprehend I just don't deal with it."

He was subtle about it, but that pastor was challenging the virgin birth. His statement implied that the virgin birth is somehow an optional or irrelevant truth. It isn't. Satan knows that, even if we don't. Perhaps that is why he has worked so hard to discredit the virgin birth.

The challenges have taken many forms, from mockery to outright denial. One recent book claimed that Jesus was the illegitimate child of a Roman soldier who had a love affair with Mary. The author cynically pointed out that Nazareth was located on the main highway between Jerusalem and the Phoenician cities of Tyre and Sidon. Nazareth, he said, was notorious for corruption, vice, and prostitution. There's nothing new about that kind of skepticism. Before he met Christ, Nathanael asked Philip: "Can any good thing come out of Nazareth?" (John 1:46).

There's nothing new about that theory of Christ's origin either. Jesus' enemies often questioned His parentage (see John 6:42; 8:41). As early as the eighth century, an extremist anti-Christian cult popularized the teaching that after Mary married Joseph, she unwittingly conceived a child by a neighbor who came in the dark of night and had sex with her. She assumed the man was Joseph and because she never saw his face in the dark, she never knew the difference. According to the legend Joseph knew he was not the father, so he left Mary after she delivered a son. Of course none of that has any basis in historical fact; its sole purpose was to make Jesus illegitimate and remove His divine nature. The antagonists who concocted the story wanted only to invalidate Jesus' claim to be Messiah.

Similar attacks have been made on the virgin birth, even in our own generation. Hugh Schoenfield in *The Passover Plot*, a popular book during the sixties, postulated that Jesus was the natural son of Joseph and Mary. Schoenfield viewed Jesus as nothing but a master conspirator who thought He could be the Messiah and purposely tried to fulfill the Messianic prophecies. Schoenfield wrote, "There was nothing peculiar about the birth of Jesus. He was not God incarnate and no virgin mother bore him. The church in its ancient zeal fathered a myth and became bound to it as dogma."*

Those attacks, coming from avowed unbelievers, are predictable. Other attacks—more dangerous because of their subtlety—have been made against the virgin birth by those who masquerade as friends of Christianity. One influential theology professor several years ago concluded that it makes no difference if the virgin birth really happened. We can view it as a myth in the highest and best sense of the word, he said. Unfortunately, this has become a popular way of thinking. Another church leader recently called the virgin birth a story on the level of an Andy Capp comic! That's okay, he hastened to add, because Andy Capp is true—he is true in our imagination, and so is the virgin birth.

That's nonsense—the virgin birth means nothing if it resides only in the collective imagination of humanity. If the virgin birth were anything less than literal in the fullest sense, Christ would be just another man. And that is what the adversaries of the virgin birth want to prove.

Another way Satan attacks the virgin birth is through counterfeits. A number of religions have claimed the equivalent of a virgin birth. For example, Greek mythology taught that Dionysus, the god of wine, was born out of the union of his human mother, Semele, and the god Zeus. In ancient Assyrian mythology, Semiramis, wife of Nimrod, gave birth to Tammuz, who was supposedly conceived by a sunbeam. That legend was absorbed into Egyptian mythology, where the two are known as Isis and Osiris. In India the same tale is told of Isi and Iswara. The Chinese have evidence of an ancient mother cult known as the Shing Moo. Their artwork, picturing the holy mother holding a baby in her arms, looks strikingly similar to Christian art portraying Mary. In Phoenicia it was Ashtoreth, and Baal was the child. One legend about the Buddha claims he was miraculously con-

---

*(New York: Bantam, 1965), 42.

ceived when an elephant entered his mother's belly. Ten months later Buddha was born. Olympias, the mother of Alexander the Great, often asserted that he was conceived by the gods.

Other, more subtle counterfeits have obscured the truth in the Christian world. Don't confuse the virgin birth with the Roman Catholic doctrine of Immaculate Conception. That is the teaching that Mary was conceived in her mother's womb as a sinless being, preserved from the effects of Adam's sin.* However, Scripture says nothing about that; it is an invention of the medieval church, not even recognized as official Catholic church dogma until Pope Pius IX declared it so in 1854.

Sadly, the doctrine of Immaculate Conception is only one more counterfeit of the virgin birth. It makes Mary's own conception and birth supernatural and elevates her to a level she does not occupy in Scripture (Matthew 12:46–50). Mary herself has become an object of veneration, contrary to the spirit of Christ's teaching (Luke 11:27–28). She has been made into a legend no different from Semiramis or Shing Moo. Such is the confusion the enemy has sown.

Some scholars who want to deny Christ's virgin birth have characterized the biblical account as just another in a long line of legends. But all the bizarre myths of human religions stand in stark contrast to the simple reality of Jesus' conception, and none of them is rooted in history.

The Importance of the Virgin Birth

You may be wondering why the virgin birth—of all the miracles in Scripture—is so frequently attacked. After all, if one can believe, say, that Moses parted the Red Sea, what's the big deal about a virgin birth? It certainly isn't as

---

*Mary was *not* sinless. We know this from the fact that she spoke of God as "my Savior" (Luke 1:47).

The Uniqueness of the Virgin Birth

In July 1978, a little girl named Louise Brown was born in England. At 5 pounds 12 ounces, Louise was a tiny baby, but what made her birth truly extraordinary was that she was the first child ever born who was conceived outside the human body. Little Louise Brown was the first "test-tube baby."

Since then, many other children have been conceived by *in vitro* fertilization. It is amazing—unthinkable just a few years ago—but it is not miraculous. Conception occurs by a male seed fertilizing a female egg. Birth occurs normally. The only difference is the place of conception.

Scientists are experimenting with other amazing techniques to enable conception and birth by other than natural means. For example, sperm and eggs may now be frozen and thawed out to conceive an *in vitro* fetus, even after years of dormancy. For years scientists have experimented with *parthenogenesis*. The name comes from two Greek words, *parthenos*, meaning "virgin," and *genesis*, meaning "beginning" or "birth." Literally, then, parthenogenesis is the science of virgin birth. Laboratory experiments have revealed that in some cases parthenogenetic life can be generated in some animals. Among honeybees, for example, the unfertilized eggs develop naturally into drones. Artificial parthenogenesis has been used to produce silkworms since 1888. Many forms of invertebrates and plants may be reproduced fairly easily through parthenogenesis. In recent years frogs and rabbits have been reproduced by parthenogenesis in laboratory experiments.

But parthenogenesis can reproduce only genetically identical species. Frog eggs, for example, might be stimulated to develop by parthenogenesis into living frogs, but all of them will be female frogs genetically identical to the mother who laid the eggs. Also, parthenogenesis, cloning, and other experimental forms of reproduction have all proved impossible on the human level.

Even in the face of modern science, Christ's conception remains unique. Science can never explain how a virgin, a woman who had never had a sexual relationship with a man, could give birth to a male child. It was a miracle of God, the greatest miracle of conception the world has ever known.

spectacular a miracle. And Scripture devotes relatively little space to describing it. Can it really be that important?

Yes. The virgin birth is an underlying assumption in *everything* the Bible says about Jesus. To throw out the virgin birth is to reject Christ's deity, the accuracy and authority of Scripture, and a host of other related doctrines that are the heart of the Christian faith. No issue is *more* important than the virgin birth to our understanding of who Jesus is. If we deny that Jesus is God, we have denied the very essence of Christianity. Everything else the Bible teaches about Christ hinges on the truth we celebrate at Christmas—that Jesus is God in human flesh. If the story of His birth is merely a fabricated or trumped-up legend, then so is the rest of what Scripture tells us about Him. The virgin birth is as crucial as the resurrection in substantiating His deity. It is not an optional truth. Anyone who rejects Christ's deity rejects Christ absolutely—even if he pretends otherwise (see 1 John 4:1–3).

Jesus Himself viewed the question of His parentage as a watershed issue. Matthew records one of the last confrontations He had with the Pharisees: "While the Pharisees were gathered together, Jesus asked them a question, saying, 'What do you think about the Christ, whose son is He?' They said to Him, 'The son of David.' He said to them, 'Then how does David in the Spirit call Him "Lord," saying, "The Lord said to my Lord, 'Sit at My right hand, Until I put Thine enemies beneath Thy feet.'" ' If David then calls Him "Lord," how is He his son?' And no one was able to answer Him a word, nor did anyone dare from that day on to ask Him another question" (22:41–46).

His sonship was the source of controversy on other occasions. John 8 records another run-in with some leading Pharisees. They told Jesus, "We were not born of fornication; we have one Father, even God" (v. 41). "We were not born of fornication" is a not-so-subtle jab at Jesus. They were implying that *He* was born illegitimately. They twisted the whole point of His miraculous birth to make Him a bastard child. They even said in verse 48, "Do we not say rightly that You are a Samaritan and have a demon?"

The fact is, there is a direct parallel between those Pharisees and the religious leaders of today who hint that the virgin birth is unimportant or a fable. Their challenges grow out of unbelief in Jesus Christ. They are the expression of sinful, unregenerate hearts.

Contrast their response with that of Peter. Matthew 16:13–17 records this exchange between Jesus and His disciples. Again, His sonship is the issue: "Jesus came into the district of Caesarea Philippi. He began asking His disciples, saying, 'Who do people say that the Son of Man is?' And they said, 'Some say John the Baptist; some, Elijah; and others, Jeremiah, or one of the prophets.' He said to them, 'But who do you say that I am?' And Simon Peter answered and said, 'Thou art the Christ, the Son of the living God.' And Jesus answered and said to him, 'Blessed are you, Simon Barjonas, because flesh and blood did not reveal this to you, but My Father who is in heaven.' "

Notice that all the answers the masses were proposing were human ones. They had concluded Jesus was either John the Baptist, Elijah, Jeremiah, or one of the prophets. They had not yet grasped the truth of His deity. Their assumption always was that He was just a man. Simon Peter's response was different. He understood that Jesus was more than a human messiah, more than an anointed prophet, more than a son of David. He was the Son of the living God. Peter knew because God had revealed it to him (v. 17). Flesh and blood cannot reach that conclusion. Science, philosophy, and human religion cannot explain who Jesus is. Their adherents will inevitably conclude that He is a great teacher, a good moral example, or even a prophet of God. But they all miss the fact that He is the Son of the living God.

That's why the virgin birth is so important. For Jesus to be God, He must be born of God. Joseph, a man, and Mary, a woman, cannot produce God. God cannot be born into this world by natural human processes. There's no way He could be God apart from being conceived by God.

The Old Testament and the Virgin Birth

The virgin birth was no afterthought in God's Messianic plans. The Old Testament prophesied it. As far back as the earliest chapters of Genesis, which record the fall of Adam and Eve, we find hints that God would send a virgin-born redeemer. After Adam and Eve disobeyed God and ate the forbidden fruit, God pronounced this curse on the serpent, Satan: "I will put enmity between you and the woman, and between your seed and her seed; He shall bruise you on the head, and you shall bruise him on the heel" (Genesis 3:15).

"Her seed" is an expression used nowhere else in Scripture. Every other time Scripture speaks of someone's offspring as "seed," it is speaking of the male seed, or sperm. Only one time does Scripture ever speak of the seed of a woman, and that's an indication of something special.

Furthermore, God said Satan would war against the woman's seed. Their enmity would culminate in a final battle. "He shall bruise you on the head, and you shall bruise him on the heel" prophesies victory to the woman's seed. We know the fulfillment. The cross was where Satan "bruised" Christ, but our Lord's death ultimately turned out to be a crushing blow to the head of Satan.

Isaiah 7:14, which we have already looked at briefly, also prophesies the virgin birth: "The Lord Himself will give you a sign: Behold, a virgin will be with child and bear a son, and she will call His name Immanuel."

Those who reject the Messianic intent of this verse point out that the Hebrew word translated "virgin" here—*almah*—

can mean "young girl."* But if this is just any young woman having a baby, that's no sign; lots of young women have babies. A sign is meant to get your attention. To be useful, a sign must be specific and unique. If, for example, you were driving and saw a sign that said, "City Limits," it wouldn't help if you didn't know what city you were entering. When God gave this sign, He was pointing to something extraordinary, something unusual.

A *virgin* bearing a son would indeed be a sign. Matthew 1:23 gives the divine interpretation of Isaiah 7:14, and there the word is translated "virgin." The Greek word in Matthew 1:23 is *parthenos,* and that can't mean anything but "virgin"— one who has known only sexual abstinence.

Jeremiah 31:22 is another Old Testament passage that hints at the virgin birth: "The Lord has created a new thing in the earth—a woman will encompass a man." Some rabbis even before the time of Christ saw Messianic meaning in that verse. "Messiah is to have no earthly father," one wrote. "The birth of Messiah will be without defect. The birth of Messiah will be like that of no other man." Another rabbi said, "The birth of Messiah will be like the dew of the Lord as drops on the grass without the action of a man."

Indeed that was how Christ was conceived—apart from any human agency.

Thus began the Christmas story. Quietly, without fanfare, God's Son was conceived in a young woman who had never known intimacy with any man. The chain of events this set off would change Mary's life—and Joseph's—forever.

More than that, the Son from on high whom she bore would alter the course of all human history in a way no one before Him had ever dreamed possible—and no one since has ever equaled. Clearly, Jesus was God's own Son.

---

*The word *almah* appears only nine times in the Old Testament, and eight of those nine the word *must* mean "virgin."

When Was the First Christmas?

No one really knows when Christ was born. It probably was *not* December 25, because Scripture says there were shepherds in the fields watching over their flocks, and that would have been highly unlikely in the middle of winter.

Our focus on December 25 came from the Roman holiday called Saturnalia. This was a pagan observance of the birthday of the unconquered sun. Saturnalia began December 19 each year, which, in the northern hemisphere, is when the days start getting longer, and continued with seven days of wild revelry. Many of our Christmas customs have their origins in Saturnalia, which was marked by feasting, parades, special music, gift giving, lighted candles, and green trees. As Christianity spread through the Roman empire, the pagan holiday was given Christian connotations. In 336 Emperor Constantine declared Christ's birthday an official Roman holiday. Some church leaders, such as Chrysostom, rebuked Christians for adopting a pagan holiday, but December 25 has endured as the date we celebrate Christ's birth.

Joseph and Mary

Mary's faith is a wonderful example for us. Rather than resentfully looking at her pregnancy as unfair and embarrassing, she understood that she had been uniquely blessed by God (Luke 1:48–49). Joseph, too, is a remarkable example of extraordinary faith. Understandably distressed when he discovered Mary was going to have a baby, he nevertheless accepted the difficult consequences of God's will for their lives. Though they must have suffered tremendously from the lies and innuendo of cruel gossip-mongers, Joseph and Mary were steadfast. They probably didn't understand the fullness of God's plan, but they followed unwaveringly. They were ideal earthly parents for God's only begotten Son.

History has romanticized Joseph and Mary. We tend to think of them as larger than life. Artists often picture them with mystic expressions and halos around their heads. In reality they were common folk. Joseph was a carpenter, and Mary was a young girl from a simple background. They could hardly have been more plain. Only their faith was extraordinary.

In all likelihood, Joseph and Mary were very young. They were probably in their teens, because marriages in their culture tended to be arranged at a young age. Betrothals often occurred when girls were as young as twelve or thirteen. What we know about Mary indicates she had reached a level

of maturity beyond most teenagers; perhaps she was in her late teens or early twenties. Joseph was probably not much older.

Their lives were forever changed when the archangel Gabriel appeared to Mary with the announcement that she would bear a son. Consider the impact that news had on them. Did you know, for example, that Joseph almost divorced Mary over her pregnancy? We can only imagine the agony and heartache he experienced when he first heard Mary was carrying a child he knew wasn't his.

The Way Mary Saw It

Luke 1:27 says Mary was engaged to Joseph. Engagement in that culture did not mean the same thing it means today. The rabbinical writings distinguish two stages in Hebrew marriage. The *kiddushin*, or betrothal period, was legally as binding as marriage. If at any time during the *kiddushin* either of the couple violated the vows or was found to be unchaste, a formal divorce was required to nullify the marriage contract. In other words, the two parties were in every sense legally married—they were even called husband and wife—but they had no physical relationship whatsoever. They lived in separate homes. The *kiddushin* was normally a twelve-month period. It was intended to prove the fidelity of both husband and wife. If either partner was unfaithful or other problems surfaced, those problems could be resolved before the marriage was consummated.

The second stage of Hebrew marriage, the *huppa*, was like a modern wedding, only a much bigger occasion. Weddings often lasted seven days. It was such a wedding in Cana where Jesus did His first miracle by turning water to wine (John 2:1–11). If the ceremony had been going on for seven days, it's little wonder that they ran short of wine!

Mary's pregnancy began during their *kiddushin*. She and

Joseph had entered into a marriage contract but were still living separately when, nine months before that first Christmas, the archangel appeared to Mary. Luke 1:26–38 records what happened:

> In the sixth month [of Elizabeth's pregnancy] the angel Gabriel was sent from God to a city in Galilee, called Nazareth, to a virgin engaged to a man whose name was Joseph, of the descendants of David; and the virgin's name was Mary. And coming in, he said to her, "Hail, favored one! The Lord is with you." But she was greatly troubled at this statement, and kept pondering what kind of salutation this might be. And the angel said to her, "Do not be afraid, Mary; for you have found favor with God. And behold, you will conceive in your womb, and bear a son, and you shall name Him Jesus. He will be great, and will be called the Son of the Most High; and the Lord God will give Him the throne of His father David; and He will reign over the house of Jacob forever; and His kingdom will have no end." And Mary said to the angel, "How can this be, since I am a virgin?" And the angel answered and said to her, "The Holy Spirit will come upon you, and the power of the Most High will overshadow you; and for that reason the holy offspring shall be called the Son of God. And behold, even your relative Elizabeth has also conceived a son in her old age; and she who was called barren is now in her sixth month. For nothing will be impossible with God." And Mary said, "Behold, the bondslave of the Lord; be it done to me according to your word." And the angel departed from her.

A supernatural, miraculous tone permeates that entire account. The angel, the Holy Spirit, the prophetic utterance, the Son of God conceived by a miracle in Mary's womb, Elizabeth's pregnancy despite the fact that she was old and formerly barren—all those elements add to the sense that something dramatic and miraculous was taking place.

Three times this passage says Mary was a virgin. There's no lack of clarity. There are no alternative translations of the Greek word used in this passage. Mary was pure and chaste, having never known any man sexually. The Bible is definite about that.

We don't know much else about Mary's background from Scripture. By comparing the gospel records, we discover that she had a sister named Salome, the mother of Zebedee's children (Matthew 27:56; Mark 15:40; John 19:25). Zebedee was the father of the apostles James and John. They were all simple fishermen (Matthew 4:21–22). Luke says Elizabeth, mother of John the Baptist, was a relative of Mary (Luke 1:36). Luke's genealogy refers to Mary's father as Eli (3:23). Other than that, we know almost nothing about Mary. Her early life was spent in Nazareth. She was probably from a poor family, and was no doubt hardworking. It is obvious she was an exceptionally virtuous and godly young woman.

The simplicity of Mary's faith is remarkable, given the circumstances. Her simple answer, "Behold, the bondslave of the Lord; be it done to me according to your word," gives us insight into her character. Quietly, modestly, submissively, she saw her role as a simple servant of the Lord. She might have been tempted to either boast or rebel, but she did neither. Luke 2:19 further reveals Mary's godly character, showing her typical response to the extraordinary work of God in her life: "Mary treasured up all these things, pondering them in her heart" (see also v. 51).

It's hard to imagine a more gracious response to the angel's announcement than Mary's. Certainly her response shows deep and mature faith. A typical woman from our culture might have said, "Joseph, I had this weird dream. I need to go see a counselor."

She simply submitted to God's plan for her. Luke 1:46–55 records her response, known as the Magnificat:

> My soul exalts the Lord, and my spirit has rejoiced in God my Savior. For He has had regard for the humble state of His bondslave; for behold, from this time on all generations will count me blessed. For the Mighty One has done great things for me; and holy is His name. And His mercy is upon generation after generation toward those who fear Him. He has done mighty deeds with His arm; He has scattered those who were proud in the thoughts of their heart. He has brought down rulers from their thrones, and has exalted those who were humble. He has filled the hungry with good things; and sent away the rich empty-handed. He has given help to Israel His servant, in remembrance of His mercy, as He spoke to our fathers, to Abraham and his offspring forever.

Those words reveal a singular faith. There was no questioning in her mind, no doubt, no misgivings, no fear, no demanding to understand—only an instant submission and the confidence that this was in fact God's truth. She expressed her heart in praise.

The Way Joseph Saw It

We know nothing about Joseph's background, either. He is called a "carpenter" (Matthew 13:55). The Greek word can be translated "woodworker" or "mason." It may have been that he did both. If he built houses he would need to be able to lay bricks and frame windows and doors too. At any rate, he worked hard for a living and probably was anything but rich.

He was a godly man of faith, however. Matthew 1:19 calls him "a righteous man." Matthew tells the story from Joseph's point of view: "The birth of Jesus Christ was as follows. When His mother Mary had been betrothed to Joseph, before they came together she was found to be with child by the Holy Spirit. And Joseph her husband, being a righteous man, and not wanting to disgrace her, desired to put her away secretly" (Matthew 1:18–19).

Poor Joseph, a just and righteous man, was deeply committed to Mary. No doubt he was looking forward to the day when they could come together as man and wife. He was jolted by the news that Mary was pregnant. He knew the quality of her character. He knew the righteous standard by which she lived. He knew her commitment to God. He knew a premarital pregnancy was totally out of character. It made no sense at all. Joseph must have felt his whole world was coming to an end.

The law of Israel demanded that a woman who became pregnant with a child outside of marriage should be put to death. Deuteronomy 22:20–21 prescribes the punishment for a newlywed woman whose husband discovers she is not a virgin: "If this charge is true, that the girl was not found a virgin, then they shall bring out the girl to the doorway of her father's house, and the men of her city shall stone her to death because she has committed an act of folly in Israel, by playing the harlot in her father's house; thus you shall purge the evil from among you." The rest of Deuteronomy 22 describes the consequences for several varieties of sexual sin outside of marriage. In almost every case, the punishment for the guilty parties is death.

So Joseph was shaken to the very core of his soul. Had they been living in Moses' day, Mary would have been immediately stoned. But the laxness of the Jewish theocracy and the infiltration of Roman law in Joseph's day gave him two other options. One, he could make her a public example. That is, he could charge her with adultery in a public court. She would be shamed, brought to trial, convicted in front of everyone, and forever ruined in terms of reputation. The other possibility was that he could quietly before two or three witnesses write a bill of divorce, and end their relationship. There would be no fanfare. Nobody would need to know. She could simply go away somewhere and secretly bear and raise the child.

Joseph loved Mary. He was torn with agony trying to decide what to do. He didn't want to make her a public example, but he couldn't marry her if she was guilty of harlotry.

He decided to divorce or put her away privately. He just couldn't bring himself to make Mary a public example. In fact, it was apparently difficult for him to decide even to put her away secretly. He must have spent considerable time thinking about it, because before he had time to act— Scripture says, "While he thought on these things" (Matthew 1:20 KJV)—the Lord intervened. Joseph was meditating, mulling over what he had to do. And while he was still pondering his options, he fell asleep.

Mary had no way to protect her reputation. She could have tried explaining to Joseph that the baby was conceived by God, but do you think he would have instantly believed her? In all of human history there had never been a virgin birth. So the Spirit of God became her advocate. The angel of the Lord appeared to Joseph in a dream and dispelled the cloud of suspicion and shame and scandal that hung ominously over Mary.

The Way God Saw It

Matthew's account of the story continues:

Behold, an angel of the Lord appeared to him in a dream, saying, "Joseph, son of David, do not be afraid to take Mary as your wife; for that which has been conceived in her is of the Holy Spirit. And she will bear a Son; and you shall call His name Jesus, for it is He who will save His people from their sins." Now all this took place that what was spoken by the Lord through the prophet might be fulfilled, saying, "Behold, the virgin shall be with child, and shall bear a Son, and they shall call His name Immanuel," which translated means, "God with us." And Joseph arose from his sleep, and did as the angel of the Lord commanded him, and took her as his wife; and kept her a virgin until she gave birth to a Son; and he called His name Jesus (Matthew 1:20–25).

Joseph's dream was not one of those where what you see isn't real. This was not some fantasy conjured up by his imagination. This was an angel—a real one, sent from God—who came to him in a vision while he was sleeping. His dream turned to reality.

The angel explained that Mary was pregnant with the son of God, and that the child she was carrying had been conceived by the Holy Spirit. That must have been more astonishing to Joseph than the original news that Mary was pregnant!

"She will bear a Son; and you shall call His name Jesus, for it is He who will save His people from their sins" (Matthew 1:21). And so, the angel told Joseph, Mary's son would come as the fulfillment of Isaiah's prophecy—virgin-born, God with us, incarnate deity—to save His people from their sins. How Joseph must have marveled! What joy there must have been when he woke up! It was the best nap Joseph ever had.

Here we see the tremendous depth and firmness of Joseph's faith. When he awoke, he took Mary as his wife. They had the *huppa,* the wedding ceremony. He spared her the shame and disgrace and loneliness of having to bear the child alone and in anonymity. He must have been a good

No Other Name Under Heaven

The angel that appeared to Joseph emphasized the meaning of Jesus' name: "She will bear a Son; and you shall call His name Jesus, for it is He who will save His people from their sins" (Matthew 1:21). *Jesus*, from the Hebrew *Joshua*, or *Jehoshua*, means "Jehovah will save." The name itself was a testimony to God's salvation. But, the angel told Joseph, Mary's Son would be the very embodiment of Jehovah's salvation. He Himself would save His people from their sins.

After Jesus' resurrection, Peter, speaking before the Sanhedrin, also emphasized the importance of Jesus' name: "There is salvation in no one else; for there is no other name under heaven that has been given among men, by which we must be saved" (Acts 4:12).

What a startling statement that is! It destroys the popular notion that there are many ways to God. There is only one way, and that is Jesus. No religion, no philosophy, no ceremony, and no good deeds can obtain salvation. Only one name under heaven has been given by which salvation is offered. It is Jesus, the One who is God with us, who came to save His people from their sins.

man. Can you imagine the Almighty God of the universe depositing His only Son in the home of a man who wasn't?

Joseph kept Mary a virgin (v. 25). Though to external appearances they were husband and wife, he had no physical relationship with her until after Jesus was born. Thus Isaiah's prophecy of a virgin birth was literally fulfilled.

One popular legend has it that Mary remained a virgin the rest of her life. That's not true. After Jesus' birth, Mary and Joseph had a normal physical relationship as husband and wife, which produced other children. The Bible even gives the names of some of Jesus' siblings (Matthew 13:55).

Imagine having someone in your family who is none other than God in human flesh! Scripture tells us very little about Jesus' early life or family. We know that even at a young age, He was occupied with His Father's business (Luke 2:49). He clearly understood who He was and why He had come—to save His people from their sin.

It's interesting to think about why God chose Mary and Joseph to give an earthly home to His Son. After all, they were working people living in Nazareth, a poor and even backward region. There was nothing sophisticated about them or their way of life. They provided the perfect environment for Jesus to grow.

When He was older, Jesus would dwell among the sick to heal them. He would walk among the demon-possessed to liberate them. He would fellowship with the poor and downtrodden and needy. He would touch lepers to make them whole. He would minister to the hungry and destitute multitudes. He would feed and heal people in need. But most of all He would seek and save the lost (Luke 19:10).

Immanuel, infinitely rich, became poor. He assumed our nature, entered our sin-polluted world, took our guilt on Himself although He was sinless, bore our griefs, carried our sorrows, was wounded with our transgressions, bruised for our iniquities. All of that is wrapped up in this phrase, "God with us."

The apostle Paul penned one of the gladdest truths in all of Scripture: "You know the grace of our Lord Jesus Christ, that though He was rich, yet for your sake He became poor, that you through His poverty might become rich" (2 Corinthians 8:9).

That's the immeasurable gift of Christmas. Christ, God's own Son, gave up His wealth and privilege to live as God with us, that He might save His people from their sins, and that we through His poverty might become rich.

The Turning Point of History

The birth of Jesus Christ, next to His crucifixion, was the most momentous event in the history of the world. It became the focal point of all history. Everything before Christ looked forward to His birth, and everything since then looks back at Him. It was such a crucial event that now all the world numbers years according to it. *B.C.* means "before Christ," and *A.D.* means "anno domini," "in the year of our Lord."

Jesus made an impact on the world that has never been, and never will be, equaled by any mere man. In all the annals of the human race, no one is like Him. He never wrote a book. He never held political power. He was not wealthy or particularly influential in His lifetime. Yet He altered the world completely; in fact, no other human being has affected history remotely like He has.

He has been opposed, hated, fought, censored, banned, and criticized in every generation since His birth. Yet His influence continues unabated. After nearly two thousand years, the impact of His life goes on so powerfully that it is safe to say not a day passes but that lives are revolutionized by His teaching.

The People Who Missed Christmas

"No room." Those shameful words describe more than the inn in Bethlehem. They apply just as aptly to today's world. Sadly, in all the busyness of our Christmas celebrations, most people still make no room for Jesus. Without even realizing it, they miss Christmas, just like most of the people in and around Bethlehem on the night Jesus was born.

Did you know most people miss Christmas every year?

That may sound rather silly, especially in North America, where during the holidays we drown in a sea of Christmas advertising. Still, I'm convinced that most people miss Christmas. They observe the season because culture says it's the thing to do, but the masses are utterly oblivious to the reality of what they are celebrating. So much fantasy and myth have been imposed on the holiday that people are numb to the real miracle of Christ's birth. The legitimate emotion of the holiday has given way to a maudlin and insincere self-indulgence. A newspaper I saw recently had a two-page spread featuring some man-on-the-street interviews where people offered their opinions of the real meaning of Christmas. The views ranged from mawkish to irreverent. Some were sentimental, saying Christmas is a family time, a time for children, and so on. Others were humanistic, seeing Christmas as a time to celebrate love for one's fellow man, the spirit of giving, and that sort of thing. Others were crassly hedonistic, viewing Christmas as just another excuse to party. Not one person made mention of the incomprehensible miracle of God's birth as a human baby.

What a mess Christmas is! We have compounded the holiday with so many traditions and so much hype and hysteria that we miss the utter simplicity of Christ's birth. It is ironic that of all holidays, this one has become the most complex. It is no wonder so many people miss Christmas.

One thing hasn't changed since the time of Joseph and Mary: nearly everyone missed that first Christmas, too. Like people today, they were busy, consumed with all kinds of things—some important, some not—but nearly everyone missed Christ. The similarities between their world and ours are striking. Every one of those people has a counterpart in modern society.

The Innkeeper

Scripture doesn't specifically mention him, but that night in Bethlehem, an innkeeper was confronted by a man and his pregnant wife. He turned them away saying he had no room for them. And so he missed Christmas. Not only did he turn Mary and Joseph away, but he apparently didn't even call for anyone to help a young mother about to give birth.

Luke 2:7 sets the scene: "[Mary] gave birth to her first-born son; and she wrapped Him in cloths, and laid Him in a manger, because there was no room for them in the inn."

That verse is explicitly concerned with a lonely birth. There are no midwives, no assistance to Mary at all. The Bible doesn't even mention that Joseph was present. Perhaps he was, but if he was typical of first-time fathers, he would have been of little help to Mary. She was basically on her own.

Such a birth was far from typical in the first-century

Bedlam

The Christmas season is marked by deeper emotional strain, greater anxiety, and more acts of violence than any other time of the year. The stress of the holiday, the depressing weight of loneliness, and the meaninglessness of mindless revelry make the holiday intolerable for many people. Observe what happens in most retail stores during the final shopping days before Christmas, and you'll understand why more people suffer nervous breakdowns at Christmas than at any other time of the year.

Ironically, the word *bedlam* itself is a corruption of *Bethlehem*. In the 1500s the priory of St. Mary of Bethlehem, a London monastery serving as a hospital, became a city-run insane asylum. For a small admission price, people could actually go there to heckle the inmates. It was, astonishingly, one of the famous tourist attractions in the city.

St. Mary of Bethlehem was shortened to Bethlehem, pronounced "bedlam." In time, the word *bedlam* came to refer to the noise and confusion that symbolized the insane asylum. And so *Bethlehem* and *bedlam* are historically and semantically related.

Jewish culture. These were not barbaric people or aboriginal tribes that sent their women off into the jungle to have their babies alone on a banana leaf. They were civilized, intelligent, educated, and above all hospitable people who cared deeply about human life. It would be highly unusual for a young woman about to give birth to be turned away from an inn and left to give birth alone in a stable.

Yet that's what happened. Mary brought forth the child, *she* wrapped Him in swaddling cloth, and *she* laid Him in a manger! Where usually a midwife would clean the baby and wrap him, there was no one. Mary did it herself. And where usually there would have been a cradle or basket for the baby, there was none. Mary had to put Him in an animal's feeding trough.

G. Campbell Morgan wrote, "Think of the pathos of it. 'She brought forth;' 'she wrapped Him in swaddling clothes.' It is very beautiful, but oh, the pity of it, the tragedy of it, the loneliness of it; that in that hour of all hours, when womanhood should be surrounded by the tenderest care, she was alone. The method of the writer is very distinct. She with her own hands wrapped the Baby round with those swaddling clothes, and laid Him in a manger. There was no one to do it for her. Again I say, the pity of it, and yet the glory of it to the heart of Mary."*

As I said, the innkeeper is not specifically mentioned. In fact, Scripture is not clear about what kind of inn Bethlehem had. The Greek word translated "inn" is *kataluma*. That can mean "guest room," "hostel," or simply "shelter." So the inn could have been anything from a full-fledged precursor of the modern bed-and-breakfast lodge to a lean-to on someone's property that was built to house both people and animals.

---

*G. Campbell Morgan, *The Gospel According to Luke* (Old Tappan, N.J.: Revell, 1929), 36.

Scripture gives no clue beyond the single mention of an inn. In any case, whatever hospitality Joseph and Mary sought, it was unavailable to them. They were turned away.

The innkeeper may have been a landowner whose property included an informal shelter, or perhaps he was the host of a boardinghouse. Whatever the case, an innkeeper in Bethlehem missed that first Christmas. The Son of God might have been born on his property. But he turned away a young mother about to deliver a child, and so he missed Christmas.

He missed it because he was preoccupied. His inn, or his guest room, or his lean-to shelter, was full. It was census time in Bethlehem (Luke 2:1–6), and the city was bulging with everyone whose ancestry went back to the little town. Bethlehem was the city of David, so every living descendant of David would have been there, along with every other family whose roots were in Bethlehem. The town was crowded. The innkeeper was busy. There is no indication that he was hostile or even unsympathetic. He was just busy, that's all.

Exactly like millions of people today. Their souls are consumed with activity—not necessarily sinful activity; just things that keep them busy. At Christmas, people are especially busy. Shopping, banquets, parties, concerts, school activities, and other things all compete for attention. And in the clutter of activity, many preoccupied people miss the Son of God.

Herod

Meet another man who missed the first Christmas: Herod. Matthew 2 tells his story. He was very different from the innkeeper. He wasn't ignorant; he was very well informed:

> After Jesus was born in Bethlehem of Judea in the days
> of Herod the king, behold, magi from the East arrived in

Jerusalem, saying, "Where is He who has been born King of the Jews? For we saw His star in the East, and have come to worship Him." And when Herod the king heard it, he was troubled, and all Jerusalem with him. And gathering together all the chief priests and scribes of the people, he began to inquire of them where the Christ was to be born. And they said to him, "In Bethlehem of Judea, for so it has been written by the prophet, 'And you, Bethlehem, land of Judah, are by no means least among the leaders of Judah; for out of you shall come forth a Ruler, who will shepherd My people Israel.'" Then Herod secretly called the magi, and ascertained from them the time the star appeared. And he sent them to Bethlehem, and said, "Go and make careful search for the Child; and when you have found Him, report to me, that I too may come and worship Him" (Matthew 2:1–8).

Herod pretended he wanted to worship Jesus Christ, but he was fearful of this One who was called the King of the Jews. He didn't want any competition for his throne. The phrase "he was troubled" (v. 3) uses a word that means "agitated, stirred up, shaken up." It conveys the idea of panic. His supremacy was in jeopardy. He had no use for any other King of the Jews.

If the innkeeper's problem was preoccupation, Herod's was fear. Herod was an Idumean; he wasn't even a Jew. His father, Antipater, had done some favors to Rome. As payment, the Herod family was given the right to rule Judea, which was under Roman occupation. Herod was a consummate politician; he continued to do everything he could to gain favor with Rome. In return the Roman senate gave him an army. Herod was able to extend his empire from Judea to Jordan to Syria to Lebanon. He even called himself "King of the Jews," and he was known by that title until his death.

It's no wonder he panicked when he heard someone else had been born who was being called King of the Jews. He was immediately threatened—even though Jesus was a baby and he was an old man.

Herod was ruthless. His chief appeal to Rome was the merciless efficiency with which he was able to extract taxes from the people. He had murdered all the Hasmoneans, the sons of the Maccabeans who had led a revolution against Greece's rule. He wanted to make sure they didn't do it again, so he simply slaughtered them all. He had ten wives and twelve children. One of his wives, Mariamne, had a brother, Aristobulus, who was the high priest. Herod was afraid of Aristobulus so he murdered him. Then he killed her too.

His paranoia was legendary. He was afraid one of his two eldest sons might take his throne, so he murdered them both. His entire life was one of plotting and execution. Five days before his death he executed his eldest son for plotting against his throne. In one of the final acts of his evil life, he had the most distinguished citizens of Jerusalem put in prison, and commanded that they be slaughtered the moment he died. "The people will not weep when I die," he said, "and I want them weeping, even if they weep over someone else." So even at his death there was a great slaughter.

Herod was such a brutal, merciless man that it is not difficult to imagine how he would choose to vent his rage when he learned a child had been born who according to prophecy was the true King of the Jews. He was furious when he realized the magi were not going to report back to him. "When Herod saw that he had been tricked by the magi, he became very enraged, and sent and slew all the male children who were in Bethlehem and in all its environs, from two years old and under, according to the time which he had ascertained from the magi. Then that which was spoken through

Jeremiah the prophet was fulfilled, saying, 'A voice was heard in Ramah, weeping and great mourning, Rachel weeping for her children; and she refused to be comforted, because they were no more' " (Matthew 2:16–18).

In his mad effort to wipe out one child, Herod had scores of children slaughtered. God had already warned Joseph and Mary, and they had fled to Egypt with Jesus (Matthew 2:13–15). So Herod failed. Not only did he miss the first Christmas, but his rebellion also propagated a great tragedy. All this was because of fear—jealous fear.

There are Herod types even in our society. Herod's fear was that someone else would take his throne. Lots of people are like him. They won't allow anything to interfere with their career, their position, their power, their ambition, their plans, or their lifestyle. They are not about to let someone else be king of their lives. They see Jesus as a threat, and so they miss Christmas.

People don't mind taking time off work to commemorate Jesus' birth. They will even embrace Him as a resource when they get in trouble. They might gladly accept Him as a spiritual benefactor. They are even willing to add Him to their lives and call themselves Christians, but not if He insists on being King. That might be a threat to their lifestyle or career, or whatever else they are hanging on to. They are as fearful and as jealous of losing their own self-determination as Herod was of losing his throne. They will guard at all costs their own priorities, their own values, their own morals. They won't come to Christ if He threatens to cramp their style. They will not accept His right to rule over them. They want to run the show.

The world is full of people who cry out, "We do not want this man to reign over us" (Luke 19:14). People want to determine their own careers, make their own decisions, master their own fate, chart their own destiny. And so we have a world of kings who are not about to bow to Jesus Christ. Such people are governed by the same kind of jealous fear that drove Herod. Like him they miss Christmas.

The Religious Leaders

A whole group of people who missed Christmas is mentioned in passing in Matthew's account of Herod's treachery. They are the religious leaders. Matthew 2:4–6 says that Herod, "gathering together all the chief priests and scribes of the people . . . began to inquire of them where the Christ was to be born. And they said to him, 'In Bethlehem of Judea, for so it has been written by the prophet, "And you, Bethlehem, land of Judah, are by no means least among the leaders of Judah; for out of you shall come forth a Ruler, who will shepherd My people Israel."'"

That is shocking. The chief priests and scribes knew exactly where Christ was to be born. These were the theologians, the minds, the brains, the pharisaical aristocracy, the religious elite of Israel. They knew Scripture well enough to quote Micah 5:2, which prophesied that Messiah would be born in Bethlehem. Yet they missed Christmas.

The Jewish people had been looking for their Messiah since Moses first prophesied that a great prophet would come (see Deuteronomy 18:15). They were waiting eagerly for a deliverer. Particularly now that they lived under Roman oppression, the entire nation longed for His coming. He was the great hope of the ages. The destiny of Israel was bound up in His coming. He was their deliverer, Messiah, Christ, the Anointed One. The intensity of their hunger is illustrated in the ministry of John the Baptist. People flocked to hear the one who had been sent to prepare the way for the Messiah.

Yet here were the theological experts, the guardians of spiritual truth in Israel, and they never even bothered to walk the few miles south to Bethlehem to find out for themselves if the Messiah indeed had been born.

Why did the religious leaders miss Christmas? Indifference. They didn't care. At least Herod feared Jesus' authority. The innkeeper could claim ignorance. The religious leader had all the facts. They just didn't care. Their Messiah was not really important to them.

If the truth were known, they felt they didn't need Him. They were self-righteous. They kept the law. They believed they were already all that God could ever ask of them. They were perfect in their own minds, sickeningly proud.

The root of indifference is always pride. These men were too busy with themselves to be concerned about Jesus. Engrossed in their own pride, their self-righteousness, their self-sufficiency, they carried on their ritual and their petty theological discussions in the confines of their own comfortable system. They had no time for the Son of God. In fact, when He began His public ministry, these men became His principle adversaries. They hated and despised Him and ultimately plotted His murder. They didn't want Him. They didn't think they needed Him.

I'm reminded of the plaintive cry of Jeremiah in Lamentations 1:12 as he watched all of Israel going down the path of destruction: "Is it nothing to all you who pass this way?" Jeremiah was saying, "How can you be so indifferent?"

Indifference is a profound sin against Christ. Sadly, it is one of the most common reactions to Him. It is typical of religious people who don't think they need a Savior. Such people think they're all right just the way they are. That is a dangerous attitude.

Jesus' primary ministry was to people who had problems and knew it. He said, "I did not come to call the righteous, but sinners" (Matthew 9:13). In other words, those who are indifferent—who don't realize they are sinners—cannot respond to His call. There may in fact be more people in our nation who ignore Christ because they don't realize how sinful they are than there are people who reject Him because they are wantonly evil and hate Him. Everywhere you look you can see indifferent people who don't care about the Savior because they don't understand their need for salvation. They don't openly oppose Him; they just ignore Him. They don't care about the remedy because they don't believe they have the disease. Such people miss Christmas.

The Inhabitants of Jerusalem

The entire city of Jerusalem missed Christmas. Luke 2:8–20 says, "In the same region there were some shepherds staying out in the fields, and keeping watch over their flock by night. And an angel of the Lord suddenly stood before them, and the glory of the Lord shone around them; and they were terribly frightened. And the angel said to them, 'Do not be afraid; for behold, I bring you good news of a great joy which shall be for all the people; for today in the city of David there has been born for you a Savior, who is Christ the Lord. And this will be a sign for you: you will find a baby wrapped in cloths, and lying in a manger.' . . . And they came in haste and found their way to Mary and Joseph, and the baby as He lay in the manger. And when they had seen this, they made known the statement which had been told them about this Child. And all who heard it wondered at the things which were told them by the shepherds. . . . And the shepherds went back, glorifying and praising God for all that they had heard and seen, just as had been told them."

Out of the whole of Jerusalem society God picked a band of shepherds to hear the news of Jesus' birth. That is intriguing, because shepherds were among the lowest and most despised social groups. The very nature of their work kept them from entering into the mainstream of Israel's society. They couldn't maintain the ceremonial washings and observe all the religious festivals and feasts. Yet these shepherds, close as they were to Jerusalem, were undoubtedly caring for sheep that someday would be used as sacrifices in the temple. How fitting it is that they were the first to know of the Lamb of God!

More significantly, they came to see Him. No one else did. Though the shepherds went back and told everyone what they had seen and heard, and though "all who heard it wondered at the things which were told them by the shepherds" (v. 18), not one other person came to see firsthand. Only some lowly shepherds did not miss Christmas; everyone else in Jerusalem did.

I find it remarkable that Christ was born in Bethlehem and almost no one in Jerusalem took notice. Bethlehem is only a few miles away—literally within walking distance—and Jesus' birth was the fulfillment of all that the nation had hoped for. But the entire city missed it.

Why did Jerusalem miss Christmas? The answer in one word may surprise you: religion. The people of Jerusalem were very religious. Jerusalem was the hub of religious activity in Israel. The Temple was there, and everyone who wanted to make a sacrifice had to come to Jerusalem. The people were so busy with religious ritual that they missed the reality. Consumed with the activity of their feasts and festivals and ceremonies, preoccupied with washings and legal minutiae and other externals, they missed the whole message.

In short, they were busy worshiping the right God in the wrong way. They were caught up in the externals of true religion, but they had abandoned the heart of their faith.

Did the Angels Sing?

One of the most popular Christmas carols of all time is "Hark! The Herald Angels Sing." Did you know Scripture does not say the angels sang? When they appeared to the shepherds, they were speaking, not singing.

In fact, there are only two times in Scripture where the angels are found singing. One is in Job 38:7. Here the message is a bit cryptic: "The morning stars sang together, and all the sons of God shouted for joy." "Morning stars" refers to the angels; the archangel Lucifer, before he fell and became Satan, was called "star of the morning, son of the dawn" (Isaiah 14:12). Job 38:7 describes the angels' singing at creation. That took place before Adam sinned—perhaps even before Lucifer fell.

Revelation 5:8–10 describes another incident when angels sing. Four living creatures—these are angels—join with twenty-four elders in singing a new song to Christ: "Worthy art Thou to take the book, and to break its seals; for Thou wast slain, and didst purchase for God with Thy blood men from every tribe and tongue and people and nation. And Thou hast made them to be a kingdom and priests to our God; and they will reign upon the earth."

So angels sang before the Fall of man, and after the curse is removed, they will sing again. In the meantime, they apparently minister without singing. It is as if they cannot sing while the earth is under God's curse.

Jesus didn't fit their system. They looked for a Messiah who would be a conquering hero, not a baby in a manger. They hoped for a leader who would support their religious system. Jesus opposed everything it stood for. The Sermon on the Mount proved that. He offered truth that would free them from the tyrannical, demanding, oppressive, legalistic religion the scribes and Pharisees had hung on the nation. But the majority of people were so established in their religion that they wouldn't listen.

People like that are the hardest to reach with the good news of salvation. They are so determined to earn their own salvation, to prove they can be righteous on their own, that they cannot see the depth of their spiritual poverty.

Religion can be a deadly trap. Ritual and rules enable people to feel spiritual when they are not. I have talked to countless people newly converted to Christ, who testify that although they were active in this or that church for years, they never truly knew the reality of salvation. Religious activity is not synonymous with genuine righteousness. Religion will damn people to hell as surely as immorality. In fact, Scripture tells us Satan's ultimate trick is to disguise himself as an angel of light (2 Corinthians 11:14). And so he can use even religion to make people miss Christmas.

The Romans

An entire empire missed Christmas. All of Rome could have shared in the Savior's birth, but they missed it. That first Christmas was set in a Roman scene. Herod, for example, was the ruler appointed by Rome. And it was a decree by Caesar Augustus that set everything in motion (Luke 2:1).

Who was Caesar Augustus? He's mentioned only once in Scripture, but he occupies an important place in the history of the Roman Empire. He was the grand-nephew of Julius Caesar. His name was Octavian; "Augustus" was a title meaning "venerable." He ruled Rome from 27 B.C. to A.D. 14.

Octavian was for the most part a benevolent ruler. He was responsible for the *pax Romana,* the era of peace between all the different parts of the Roman Empire. He instituted numerous reforms designed to do away with the worst forms of corruption and keep peace throughout the empire. But Octavian took the title of Pontifex Maximus, which means "highest priest." He also promoted emperor worship in the provinces.

Octavian had come to power when Julius Caesar was assassinated. In his will, Caesar left all his possessions, including the throne, to his grand-nephew. In the middle of his reign, Octavian ordered a worldwide census. That was the decree spoken of in Luke 2:1.

And so Jesus was born in the heyday of the Roman Empire. Yet nearly all of Rome missed Christmas. Roman soldiers must have been everywhere in Bethlehem and the surrounding area, overseeing the census, registering people, and keeping order. Yet they missed Jesus' birth. Why? Idolatry. They had their own gods—they were even willing to let their emperor pretend to be God. Christ did not fit into their pantheon. No mythological god could coexist with Him anyway. So the Romans totally ignored His birth. This newborn baby became just one more number in their census.

Paganism has a strong a grip on our world today, and millions miss Christmas because of it. I'm not talking only about the dark paganism of distant lands, where Christ is unknown and unheard of, and where Christmas is unheard of. Obviously, those people miss Christmas, too. But there is another, subtler, form of idolatry even in our society. And millions miss Christmas because of it. Most people in North

America don't worship carved idols or follow demonic superstition like the Romans did, but they nevertheless worship false gods. Some people worship money. Others worship sex. I know people who worship cars, boats, houses, power, prestige, popularity, and fame. Those things are pagan gods. The idolatry of the twentieth century is selfishness and materialism. If that is what you worship, you'll miss Christmas.

The People of Nazareth

Finally, and perhaps saddest of all, Nazareth missed Christmas. Nazareth was a crude, uncultured town, quite a distance from Bethlehem. The people of that region had a reputation for violence. Nathanael expressed the prevailing opinion of that little town: "Can any good thing come out of Nazareth?" (John 1:46).

Yet Nazareth was the home of Mary and Joseph, and the boyhood home of Jesus. Although He was born in Bethlehem, He grew up in Nazareth, and lived His perfect life before all the people there. Yet they completely overlooked Him. Luke 4 describes the most important Sabbath day Nazareth ever had:

> He [Jesus] came to Nazareth, where He had been brought up; and as was His custom, He entered the synagogue on the Sabbath, and stood up to read. And the book of the prophet Isaiah was handed to Him. And He opened the book, and found the place where it was written, "The Spirit of the Lord is upon Me, because He anointed Me to preach the gospel to the poor. He has sent Me to proclaim release to the captives, and recovery of sight to the blind, to set free those who are downtrodden, to proclaim the favorable year of the Lord." And He closed the book, and gave it back to the attendant, and sat down; and the eyes of all in the synagogue were fixed upon Him. And He began to say

to them, "Today this Scripture has been fulfilled in your hearing" (4:16–21).

After years of living among these people, Jesus was revealing to the Nazarenes who He was. For the first time ever, He was telling them publicly that He was the Messiah. And what was their reaction?

> All were speaking well of Him, and wondering at the gracious words which were falling from His lips; and they were saying, "Is this not Joseph's son?" And He said to them, "No doubt you will quote this proverb to Me, 'Physician, heal yourself; whatever we heard was done at Capernaum, do here in your home town as well.'" And He said, "Truly I say to you, no prophet is welcome in his home town. But I say to you in truth, there were many widows in Israel in the days of Elijah, when the sky was shut up for three years and six months, when a great famine came over all the land; and yet Elijah was sent to none of them, but only to Zarephath, in the land of Sidon, to a woman who was a widow. And there were many lepers in Israel in the time of Elisha the prophet; and none of them was cleansed, but only Naaman the Syrian." And all in the synagogue were filled with rage as they heard these things; and they rose up and cast Him out of the city, and led Him to the brow of the hill on which their city had been built, in order to throw Him down the cliff. But passing through their midst, He went His way (Luke 4:22–30).

The people who knew Jesus best—those with whom He had grown up and among whom He had lived—tried to kill Him! That's what I call missing Christmas. "He came to His own, and those who were His own did not receive Him," John 1:11 says. The people of Nazareth, who knew Him better than anyone, had no idea who He really was. Mark 6:6 says even Jesus wondered at their unbelief.

What was their problem? Familiarity. They knew Him *too* well. They knew Him so well they couldn't believe He was anyone special. Familiarity mixed with unbelief is a deadly thing. Whenever people tell me they were raised in a Christian home but have rejected the faith, I cringe. Familiarity strangles conviction. Perhaps the most tragic sin of all is the unbelief of a person who has heard all the sermons, sat through all the Bible lessons, knows all the Christmas stories, but rejects Christ. There is no gospel, no good news, for such a person, because he already knows and rejects the truth that could set him free (see Hebrews 10:26–31). What a sad way to miss Christmas!

No one has to miss Christmas. Ignorant preoccupation, jealous fear, prideful indifference, religious ritual, false gods, and even contemptuous familiarity all are merely different expressions of the one main reason people miss Christmas: unbelief.

Perhaps you've been missing Christmas. You may get presents, eat a big dinner, and decorate a tree, but you know in your heart that you are no different from the innkeeper, Herod, the religious leaders, the people of Jerusalem, the Romans, or the citizens of Nazareth. You are missing the reality of Christmas.

You don't have to miss another one. Turn from your sin and unbelief and receive Christ as Lord and God. He will forgive your sin, change your life, and give you the greatest Christmas gift anyone can receive: "He came to His own, and those who were His own did not receive Him. But as many as received Him, to them He gave the right to become children of God, even to those who believe in His name" (John 1:11–12).

Don't miss Christmas this year!

What Child Is This?

Some say He was just a good teacher,
  but good teachers don't claim to be God.

Some say He was merely a good example,
  but good examples don't mingle with prostitutes
  and sinners.

Some say He was a madman,
  but madmen don't speak the way He spoke.

Some say He was a crazed fanatic,
  but crazed fanatics don't draw children to themselves or attract men of intellect like Paul or Luke
  to be their followers.

Some say He was a religious phony,
  but phonies don't rise from the dead.

Some say He was only a phantom,
  but phantoms can't give their flesh and blood to
  be crucified.

Some say He was only a myth,
  but myths don't set the calendar for history.

Jesus has been called the ideal man, an example of love,
the highest model of religion, the foremost pattern of
virtue, the greatest of all men, and the finest teacher who
ever lived. All of those descriptions capture elements of
His character, but they all fall short of the full truth.
The apostle Thomas expressed it perfectly when he saw
Jesus after the resurrection, and exclaimed, "My Lord
and My God!" (John 20:28).

God in a Manger

The world is happy to let Jesus Christ be a baby in a manger, but not willing to let Him be the sovereign King and Lord that He is. Yet that is the central truth of the Christmas story: the Child of Christmas is God.

Lots of people who would otherwise gladly embrace Jesus as Messiah don't want Him to be God. They will welcome Him as a son of David, but not as the Son of God. They don't mind celebrating the birth of a baby, but they don't want to hear about the Lord of lords. They sing of His nativity but brazenly reject His authority. They adore Him as an infant but will not pay homage to Him as the God-man. They can tolerate the trappings of Christmas—a manger, shepherds, wise men, and Joseph and Mary—but they cannot bear the advent of God in human flesh. Consequently the world ignores the core of all Christmas truth. And instead of honoring Jesus at Christmas, they are actually mocking Him.

The enemy must love the world's Christmas celebration. He must revel in the blatant sin and blasphemy and rejection of Christ—all by people who suppose they are celebrating His birth! He must glory in the way people inoculate themselves against the truth of Christ by commemorating His birth with lip service while ignoring the point of it all—that Jesus is almighty God.

The Incarnation of God

I said in an earlier chapter that Christmas is not about the Savior's infancy; it is about His deity. The humble birth of Jesus Christ was never intended to be a facade to conceal the reality that God was being born into the world. But the modern world's version of Christmas does just that. And consequently for the greater part of humanity, Christmas has no legitimate meaning at all.

I don't suppose anyone can ever fathom what it means for God to be born in a manger. How does one explain the Almighty stooping to become a tiny infant? It was, of course, the greatest condescension the world has ever known or will ever know. Our minds cannot begin to understand what was involved in God's becoming a man. We will never comprehend why He who was infinitely rich would become poor, assume a human nature, and enter into a world He knew would reject Him and kill Him.

Nor can anyone explain *how* God could become a baby. Yet He did. Without forsaking His divine nature or diminishing His deity in any sense, He was born into our world as a tiny infant.

People often ask me if I think He cried, or if He needed the normal care and feeding one would give any other baby. Of course He did. He was fully human, with all the needs and emotions that are common to every human.

Yet He was also fully God—all wise and all powerful. How can both things be true? I don't know. But the Bible clearly teaches that it is so. In some sense, Jesus voluntarily suspended the full application of His divine attributes. He didn't give up being God, but He willingly gave up the independent use of the privileges and powers that were His as God (Philippians 2:5–8). He chose to subjugate His will to His Father's will (John 5:30; 6:38). Through all that He remained fully God.

For nearly 2,000 years, debate has been raging about who Jesus really is. Cults and skeptics have offered various explanations. They'll say He is one of many gods, a created being, a high angel, a good teacher, a prophet, and so on. The common thread of all such theories is that they make Jesus less than God.

But let the Bible speak for itself. John's gospel begins with a clear statement that Jesus is God: "In the beginning was the Word, and the Word was with God, and the Word was God. He was in the beginning with God. All things came into being by Him; and apart from Him nothing came into being that has come into being" (John 1:1–3). Who is "the Word" spoken of in these verses? Verse 14 removes any doubt: "The Word became flesh, and dwelt among us, and we beheld His glory, glory as of the only begotten from the Father, full of grace and truth."

The biblical evidence is overwhelming that this child in the manger was the incarnation of God. For one thing, He was omniscient. John 2:24–25 says that, "Jesus, on His part . . . knew all men, and because He did not need anyone to bear witness concerning man for He Himself knew what was in man." Nathanael was shocked to discover that Jesus knew all about him before they ever met. It was enough to persuade him that Jesus was the Messiah (John 1:48–50). John 4 describes Jesus' meeting with a Samaritan woman at Jacob's well. He knew everything about her (vv. 17–19, 29).

He also did the works of God, saying, "believe Me that I am in the Father, and the Father in Me; otherwise believe on account of the works themselves (John 14:11). Jesus' works are convincing proof that He is God. He began His miraculous ministry with a simple act—He created wine at a wedding in Cana (John 2:1–11). Only God can create. Moreover, He healed people who were hopelessly ill. He gave a blind man eyes. He opened ears that had never heard. He restored withered limbs. He created enough fish and bread to feed thousands. He raised the dead by simply commanding them to come forth from the grave.

The Fullness of God

There has never been another person like Jesus Christ. All the New Testament underscores that, repeatedly stressing Jesus' deity. But let me point to one passage in particular, written by the apostle Paul, which captures the essence of Jesus' divine nature. These are the truths that make Christmas truly wonderful:

> He is the image of the invisible God, the first-born of all creation. For by Him all things were created, both in the heavens and on earth, visible and invisible, whether thrones or dominions or rulers or authorities—all things have been created by Him and for Him. And He is before all things, and in Him all things hold together. He is also head of the body, the church; and He is the beginning, the first-born from the dead; so that He Himself might come to have first place in everything. For it was the Father's good pleasure for all the fulness to dwell in Him, and through Him to reconcile all things to Himself, having made peace through the blood of His cross; through Him, I say, whether things on earth or things in heaven (Colossians 1:15–20).

Paul was writing to the Christians at Colossae. The city was under the influence of a false teaching that later developed into what was known as *gnosticism*. This was the product of an elitist, heavily intellectual cult who fancied themselves the only ones who had access to the truth. The truth, they believed, was so complex that common people couldn't know it. They taught among other things the philosophical dualism that matter is evil and spirit is good. They believed that because God is a spirit, He is good, but

He could never touch matter, which is evil. Therefore they also concluded that God couldn't be the Creator of the physical universe, because if God made matter, He would be responsible for evil. And they taught that God could never become a man, because as a man He would have to dwell in a body made of evil matter.

So they postulated a different theory of creation. They taught that in the beginning God begot only spiritual beings, called emanations. Those beings begot others, and so on, in an infinite cycle of lesser beings, until finally somewhere along the line the successive emanations evolved from spirit to matter and therefore from good to evil.

These pre-gnostics taught that Jesus was one of the very early spiritual emanations of God. They believed His body couldn't be real; that would mix good and evil. So they explained away the incarnation by saying that Jesus was a good angel whose body was only an illusion. This teaching and others like it were pervasive in the early church; many of the New Testament epistles specifically refute developing gnostic ideas. In fact, the apostle John was attacking the foundation of gnostic teaching when he wrote "By this you know the Spirit of God: every spirit that confesses that Jesus Christ has come in the flesh is from God; and every spirit that does not confess Jesus is not from God" (1 John 4:2).

Incipient gnosticism is also what the apostle Paul was countering in his epistle to the Colossians. When he writes, for example, that "by Him all things were created, both in the heavens and on earth, visible and invisible, whether thrones or dominions or rulers or authorities—all things have been created by Him and for Him" (Colossians 1:16), he is refuting that same heresy. In doing so, he specifically affirms that Jesus is God in the flesh—the Creator of everything. We'll return for a closer look at Jesus' role in creation. For now we simply note that it proves He is fully God in every conceivable way.

The Image of God

Ironically, some of the cults that deny Jesus' deity try to use Colossians 1:15–20 as support for their view. They suggest, for example, that the phrase "the image of the invisible God" (v. 15) hints that Jesus was merely a created being who bore the image of God. But Genesis 1:27 says that is true of all humanity. We were created in God's likeness. We bear His mark. We only resemble Him. Jesus, on the other hand, is God's exact image.

The Greek word translated "image" here is *eikon*. It means a perfect replica, a precise copy, a duplicate—something even more like the original than a photograph. Paul is saying that God Himself is fully manifest in the Person of His Son, who is none other than Jesus Christ. He is the exact image of God. As He said Himself, "He who has seen Me has seen the Father" (John 14:9).

Hebrews 1 parallels Colossians 1:15–20 at a number of key points. Both passages explicitly teach that Jesus is God. Regarding the statement that Christ is the image of God (Colossians 1:15), for example, Hebrews 1:3 makes an identical affirmation: "He is the radiance of His glory and the exact representation of His nature." Christ is to God as the warm brilliance of light is to the sun. He brings God from a cosmic location to the very hearts of men and women. He gives light and life. He reveals God's very essence. Just as the sun was never without its brightness, so it is with Christ and God. They cannot be divided, and neither has ever existed without the other. They are one (John 10:30).

Scripture repeatedly says God is invisible. "No man has seen God at any time" (John 1:18). God told Moses, "You cannot see My face, for no man can see Me and live!"

(Exodus 33:20). Jesus said, "God is spirit, and those who worship Him must worship in spirit and truth" (John 4:24). And, "You have neither heard His voice at any time, nor seen His form" (John 5:37). Paul, writing to Timothy, called God invisible (1 Timothy 1:17). And here in Colossians 1:15, Paul also describes God as invisible.

But through Christ the invisible God has been made visible. God's full likeness is revealed in Jesus. Colossians 1:19 takes that truth a step further: "It was the Father's good pleasure for all the fulness to dwell in Him." He is not just an outline of God; He is fully God. Colossians 2:9 is even more explicit: "In Him all the fulness of Deity dwells in bodily form." Nothing is lacking. No attribute is absent. He is God in the fullest possible sense, the perfect image.

The First-born of God

In Colossians 1:15, Paul says Jesus is "the first-born of all creation." Those who reject the deity of Christ have made much of that phrase, assuming it means Jesus was a created being. But the word translated "first-born" is *prototokos*. It describes Jesus' rank, not His origin. The firstborn, the *prototokos*, in a Hebrew family was the heir, the ranking one, the one who had the rights of inheritance. And in a royal family, the *prototokos* had the right to rule.

What this verse is saying then is that Christ is the One who inherits all creation and the right to rule over it. It doesn't mean He was born first in order, for He wasn't. The Old Testament illustration of this is the account of Jacob and Esau. Esau was born first but Jacob was the heir, the *prototokos*.

In Psalm 89:27, God says of David, "I also shall make him My first-born, The highest of the kings of the earth." There the meaning of "first-born" is given in plain language: "the highest of the kings of the earth." That's what *prototokos* means with regard to Christ—He is "King of kings and Lord of lords," to use the language of 1 Timothy 6:15 and Revelation 19:16.

Hebrews 1 again has a parallel statement. Verse 2 says God has appointed His son "heir of all things." He is the primary One, the Son who has the right to the inheritance, the ranking Person, the Lord of all, heir of the whole of creation.

The Arm of God

The claim that "first-born" means Christ is a created being completely ignores the context of Colossians 1:15. Remember, as we have noted already, verses 16–17 explicitly name Him as creator of everything: "By Him all things were created, both in the heavens and on earth, visible and invisible, whether thrones or dominions or rulers or authorities—all things have been created by Him and for Him. And He is before all things, and in Him all things hold together." Christ is not a mere part of creation; He is the Creator, the very arm of God, active from the beginning in calling the universe and all creatures into existence. John 1:2–3 says, "He was in the beginning with God. All things came into being by Him; and apart from Him nothing came into being that has come into being." That could not be true if He were Himself a created being.

Once again we can go to Hebrews 1 for confirmation of this truth. Verse 2 identifies Christ as the One through whom the world was made. Christ then is not only the heir of creation; He was also in the beginning the divine agent of creation, the Person of the Trinity through whom the world was made and for whom it was fashioned.

Think of what that means. The expanse of creation is staggering. Do you ever reflect on the size of the universe? If it doesn't give you a majestic idea of God, you haven't really considered it. A hollow ball the size of our sun, for example, would hold 1,200,000 planets the size of the earth—with room for 4,300,000 more globes the size of our moon! The nearest star, Alpha Centauri, is five times larger than the sun. Betelguese, one of the stars visible in the constellation Orion, is 248 times larger than our sun. Arcturus is more than ten times larger than that! No wonder Job expressed his awe of God this way: "How should man be just with God? If he will contend with him, he cannot answer him . . . which maketh Arcturus, Orion, and Pleiades" (Job 9:1–2, 9 KJV).

A ray of light travels at 186,000 miles a second, so a beam of light from here will reach the moon in a second and a half. Imagine you could travel that fast. You could reach Mercury in four-and-a-half minutes. Getting to Jupiter would take about 35 minutes. If you decided to go on, you could get to Saturn in about an hour, but it would take you 4 years and 4 months to get to the nearest star. Traveling just to the edge of our galaxy, the Milky Way, would take you about 100,000 years. If you could count the stars as you travel, you would find about a hundred billion in the Milky Way alone. If you wanted to explore other galaxies, you would have literally billions to choose from. The size of the universe is incomprehensible.

Who made all that? Well, say scientists, there was this big explosion that eventually formed a primordial swamp, and . . .

They cannot explain it. *God* created it all.

Who?

The babe in Bethlehem. He made everything.

Furthermore, "in Him all things hold together" (Colossians 1:17). Hebrews 1 again confirms Colossians 1. It says that Christ "upholds all things by the word of His power" (v. 3). Without Him, the whole world would fall apart. Don't buy the lie of deism, which says that God made everything, wound it up, and went away. Far from deserting His creation, He stepped into it as a little infant with only a manger for His cradle.

The Lamb of God

Who was this child? God. We see that clearly now. But why would God become a man and be born in such a lowly manner and let men treat Him the way they did? Why would Jesus, though "He is before all things" (Colossians 1:17), and though he takes "first place in everything" (v. 18), deign to come to earth as a baby, suffer the abuse He suffered, and die such a painful death? The apostle Paul tells us clearly: "It was the Father's good pleasure . . . through Him to reconcile all things to Himself, having made peace through the blood of His cross" (vv. 19–20).

He did it to make peace between God and humanity. All of us have sinned, and we sin repeatedly: "There is none righteous, not even one" (Romans 3:10). "All have sinned and fall short of the glory of God" (Romans 3:23). God hates sin and must respond with His wrath. He is a righteous judge who "is angry with the wicked every day" (Psalm 7:11 KJV). The human race reacts with more hatred, rebellion, or indifference toward God: "There is no fear of God before their eyes" (Romans 3:18). The only possible response of a holy God to our sin is more than we can bear, for "the wages of sin is death" (Romans 6:23). "If a man does not repent, He will sharpen His sword; He has bent His bow and made it ready" (Psalm 7:12).

Only Jesus, because He alone is both God and man, could ever resolve the conflict. He lived as a man, but without sin, suffering every temptation common to man, so He could be our sympathetic high priest: "We do not have a high priest who cannot sympathize with our weaknesses, but One who has been tempted in all things as we are, yet without sin"

(Hebrews 4:15). And though he was without sin, He died as a sacrifice, the spotless Lamb of God (John 1:29), an offering bearing *our* sin: "Christ also, having been offered once to bear the sins of many, shall appear a second time for salvation without reference to sin, to those who eagerly await Him" (Hebrews 9:28). Thus "having been made perfect, He became to all those who obey Him the source of eternal salvation" (Hebrews 5:9). In other words, He takes the hand of a repentant, yielding sinner and the outstretched hand of a holy yet loving God, and He joins the two. He can forgive our sins, reconcile us to God, and thus "make peace through the blood of His cross" (Colossians 1:20). And God is not reluctant for that to occur; rather it is the very reason He sent Christ into the world!

God is justifiably angry with humanity's sin. Yet He loves us enough that He gave His own son to live on earth, die on a cross, and bear our sins in His own body, suffering the full weight of God's wrath, which should have been *our* lot. He paid our penalty and restored peace between us and God. It could not have been done any other way.

The Gift of God

And so Christmas is first of all a celebration of God's love toward man. The babe in a manger is more than just a tender child. He is the image of God, the *prototokos*. He took on a body of human flesh so that He might bear in that body the sins of the world. He made possible the gift of God— eternal life (Romans 6:23). That is the sum of the Christmas message.

Don't get lost in the scope of it all. The incarnation of God in Jesus Christ is nothing if it is not personal. God loves *you*, individually. He knows you better than you know yourself, yet He loves you. He entered this world, took on human flesh, and died on a cross to bear *your* sin, to pay the penalty for *your* iniquity, to remove *your* guilt. He did it so that *you* might enter into His presence.

You must respond.

Paul wrote, "Even if our gospel is veiled, it is veiled to those who are perishing, in whose case the god of this world has blinded the minds of the unbelieving, that they might not see the light of the gospel of the glory of Christ, who is the image of God. . . . For God, who said, 'Light shall shine out of darkness,' is the One who has shone in our hearts to give the light of the knowledge of the glory of God in the face of Christ" (2 Corinthians 4:3–6).

In other words, although Christ is the revelation of God's glory, the image (*eikon*) of God, not everyone sees it. The enemy blinds the minds of unbelievers. The truth of the gospel is hid from them. It doesn't have to be. God, who in creation dispelled the darkness by merely commanding the light to shine, can cause the light of His glory to shine in your heart.

He calls you to respond in faith. Turn from your sin to Him. "The Lord is not slow about His promise [to judge the earth] . . . but is patient toward you, not wishing for any to perish but for all to come to repentance" (2 Peter 3:9). Believe Him, and trust Him with your life. "He who believes in Him is not judged; he who does not believe has been judged already, because he has not believed in the name of the only begotten Son of God. . . . He who believes in the Son has eternal life; but he who does not obey the Son shall not see life, but the wrath of God abides on him" (John 3:18, 36). Give yourself without reservation to follow Him. He must take His rightful place as Lord—"first place in everything" (Colossians 1:18). He who created everything will make you a new creature, remolded in His image, with new desires and a new heart. "Therefore if any man is in Christ, he is a new creature; the old things passed away; behold, new things have come" (2 Corinthians 5:17). Your life will never be the same.

And this Christmas will truly be a time to celebrate, for you will have the greatest gift you can ever receive, "being justified as a gift by His grace through the redemption which is in Christ Jesus" (Romans 3:24).

The Fullness of Time

The first Christmas was perfectly timed. Galatians 4:4–5 says, "When the fulness of the time came, God sent forth His Son, born of a woman, born under the Law, in order that He might redeem those who were under the Law." What was "the fulness of the time"? God's sovereign timing. He ordered world events so everything was ready for Christ's coming and the subsequent outreach of the apostles.

Looking back at the early church, we are amazed at how quickly the gospel spread in less than a century. The sovereign hand of God is clearly evident. Christ's advent could not have been timed more propitiously.

Politically, the Roman Empire was at its height. Rome had given the world good roads, a relatively fair system of government, and most important, peace. For the first time in history, people could travel with relative ease almost anywhere in the empire—and the apostles could carry the gospel message to the uttermost parts of the world.

Culturally, the world was becoming more unified. More people than ever were being educated, and most of them knew Greek or Latin. Even the common people usually spoke Koine Greek, the dialect that the New Testament was written in.

Spiritually, the world was diverse, but open. Greek and Roman polytheism were gradually being replaced by rational and secular philosophies, or by emperor worship. Among the Jews, a renewed interest in the Scriptures was leading to revival on the one hand, typified by the ministry of John the Baptist, and a strong pharisaic movement on the other. Christ could not have arrived on the scene at a more opportune time. It was the perfect time, sovereignly determined by God—"the fulness of the time."

Who Were the Wise Men?

The wise men, or magi, *are surely the strangest characters in the Christmas story. How much do you really know about them? How many were there? Were they really kings? Did they really ride camels? How did they know to come looking for the King of the Jews, when even the Jewish scholars didn't? Unfortunately, most of our conceptions about them come from the imaginations of people who draw Christmas cards. Yet what little we can gather from history indicates the magi may have been even more bizarre and exotic than most people suppose. They are one more remarkable element in the story of that first Christmas.*

In Matthew's account of Jesus' birth, we briefly meet a band of travelers who have mystified and fascinated Bible students for centuries: "After Jesus was born in Bethlehem of Judea in the days of Herod the king, behold, magi from the East arrived in Jerusalem, saying, 'Where is He who has been born King of the Jews? For we saw His star in the East, and have come to worship Him'" (Matthew 2:1–2).

The magi—called "wise men" in the King James Version—seem to materialize out of nowhere. As characters in the Christmas story, they almost seem incongruous. Matthew gives practically no details about them—what country they came from, what system of belief they represented, or how they knew the meaning of the star they had seen. They just show up, leave their gifts, and disappear.

Unfortunately, most of the popular notions about the magi are misleading. It is doubtful that they were anything like the camel-riding travelers we usually see portrayed in pictures and Christmas pageants. Even the old standard Christmas song "We Three Kings of Orient Are" may be wrong on several counts. There's no evidence that there were three of them—only that they brought three kinds of gifts (Matthew 2:11). Furthermore, Scripture does not say they were kings; in fact, they almost certainly were not. And as for their being Oriental, we simply have no information from Matthew about their origin, other than that they came "from the east." Of course, that *could* mean their home was east Asia, or even India. A Portuguese epic, the Lusiads, first published in 1572, identifies the magi as ancient Hindu brahmins. But there is no historical data to support that. In fact, as we'll see, history indicates the magi probably came instead from the land of the Medes and Persians.

All manner of notions about the magi have been advanced. Marvin R. Vincent, who wrote a series of very helpful word studies, writes, "Many absurd traditions and guesses respecting these visitors to our Lord's cradle have found their way into popular belief and into Christian art. They were said to be kings, and three in number; they were said to be representatives of the three families of Shem, Ham and Japhet, and therefore one of them is pictured as an Ethiopian; their names are given as Caspar, Balthasar, and Melchior, and their three skulls, said to have been discovered in the twelfth century by Bishop Reinald of Cologne, are exhibited in a priceless casket in the great cathedral of that city."*

Of course, it is highly improbable that those skulls,

Word Studies in the New Testament (Grand Rapids: Eerdmans, 1946), 1:19–20.

The First Christmas Cards

The original Christmas card is thought to have been sent by a British army officer named Dobson in 1844.

The first commercially produced Christmas cards were sold in England by Sir Henry Cole and J. C. Horsley in 1846. Those first cards outraged Christians, because they portrayed a group of people drinking. It was at least twenty-five years before Christmas cards were widely used.

Since then, cards have become a major industry. This year Americans alone will spend nearly one billion dollars on Christmas cards, not counting postage.

which appeared more than a thousand years after the fact, actually belonged to any magi. It is also most unlikely that any of them were Ethiopians; an Ethiopian would have to travel from the south, not from the east, to reach Bethlehem. Nor does anyone really know the names of the magi who visited the infant Christ. None of that information was recorded. Any stories that purport to give such details are only fanciful legends.

We can, however, glean some information about the magi from historical and biblical sources. What we discover is that the truth about these mysterious visitors may be even more peculiar than some of the legends.

Magi in the Old Testament World

The ancient Greek historian Herodotus records that the magi were a priestly caste of the Medes.* They were active throughout Babylon and Mesopotamia during much of the Old Testament era. The original magi were priests of the most ancient form of Zoroastrianism. The principle element of their worship was fire. They had a fire-altar that burned with a perpetual flame, which they believed had originally come down from heaven. In the sixth century B.C., Zoroastrianism became the official religion of Persia. It was still the main religion throughout Mesopotamia at the time of Jesus' birth. Zoroastrianism is still practiced today in India by the Parsees—Persians who fled their land in the seventh century A.D. to avoid Moslem persecution. The modern Parsees, therefore, are direct descendants of the magi.

The religious teachings of the magi had some striking parallels to Judaism. They were monotheistic, and they

---

*The Medes occupied the land east of Palestine and south of the Caspian sea, where Iran is today.

offered blood sacrifices, which were roasted on the altar and eaten by the worshiper and the priests. Their priesthood was hereditary, like the Levitical priesthood. They believed like the Israelites that certain insects and reptiles were unclean. They had specific rituals governing how to touch and dispose of dead bodies.

But the similarities were only counterfeits. The religion of the magi was, at its heart, satanic, based on superstition and fear, not on truth revealed by God. Unlike the Levitical priests of Judaism, the magi observed numerous demonic practices—sorcery, astrology, wizardry, divination of dreams, and other forms of soothsaying and witchcraft strictly forbidden in the Bible. They were, in short, occult practitioners. Our word *magic* comes from their name.

Of course, the ancient world made little distinction between superstition and science. The science of astronomy, for example, was blended imperceptibly with the superstition of astrology. The magi were expert in both. They were considered the scholars of their time—the wise men. No Persian could become king unless he mastered the scientific and religious discipline of the magi. Their teachings became known as "the law of the Medes and the Persians" (cf. Esther 1:19; Daniel 6:8, 12, 15). It was seen as the highest, unalterable legal code. And so in addition to being the oracles of their religion, they served as the scientists, mathematicians, philosophers, doctors, and legal authorities of their culture. Our word *magistrate* is another direct descendent of *magi*.

The magi, esteemed for their amazing intuition, wisdom, knowledge, astrology, and occult ability, rose to places of prominence in the Babylonian, Medo-Persian, and Greek empires. They acted as advisors to kings, interpreting dreams and otherwise divining wisdom through their occult magic. They also helped settle questions of science and law. Their heyday lasted from about the sixth century B.C. through the time of Christ.

Magi are mentioned in the Old Testament. Jeremiah 39:3 refers to "Nergal-sar-ezer the Rab-mag," or the chief magi in Nebuchadnezzar's court. Magi are also mentioned several times in Daniel (1:20; 2:2; 4:7; 5:11), where again they are seen serving in Nebuchadnezzar's court. That may be an important clue to understanding how the magi of Jesus' day knew to anticipate His birth.

Nebuchadnezzar was the Babylonian king who destroyed Jerusalem and the Temple and took the Jewish nation into captivity in 587 B.C. He hand-picked choice young men of extraordinary wisdom, including Daniel, Shadrach, Meshach, and Abed-nego. These he assigned to serve in his court, and they became in a sense the magi's rivals (Daniel 1:5–7).

Ironically, Daniel made an early favorable impression on Nebuchadnezzar by doing what the magi were supposed to be best at—interpreting a dream. Nebuchadnezzar had a dream that troubled his spirit, but he forgot the dream. The magi, of course, could not recover the forgotten dream for him. Nebuchadnezzar angrily ordered that all his wise men— the magi and his other soothsayers, and even Daniel—be killed. Daniel prayed, and God revealed the secret dream along with its prophetic interpretation to him. Daniel told it to the king and thus saved his own life and the lives of all the magi (Daniel 2).

Because of this extraordinary miracle, Daniel was elevated in Nebuchadnezzar's court. The king made Daniel the master of the magi (v. 48). Daniel would have then become very influential among them. Knowing what we know of his character and zeal for God, we can be certain that Daniel would have taken advantage of the opportunity to instruct the magi about the true God. It stands to reason that they would have gained a great deal of familiarity with Jewish

Scripture—including all prophecy regarding the Messiah.

Furthermore, other godly Jews in the Babylonian captivity undoubtedly shared their knowledge of the Old Testament—maybe even handmade copies of Scripture—with people all over the empire. We know that when the decree of Cyrus finally came, allowing them to go back to their own land, most Jews never did. They stayed in Babylon. Some of them even intermarried, and the history of Babylon and Medo-Persia records that many people in the noble families and high-ranking offices had at least part Jewish ancestry. No doubt many teachings and prophecies from Jewish Scripture found their way into the teachings of other religions—including those of the magi.

Magi in the Time of Christ

No one can know for sure how much Old Testament truth came into the magi's teaching, but there was ample opportunity for them to learn from Daniel and the other dispersed Jews. It seems evident that whatever truth from the Hebrews filtered into their system, much of it survived until the time of Christ. And so we find magi at the birth of Christ, familiar with Messianic prophecy and seeking the true God. More specifically, they were looking for the One who had been born King of the Jews.

The magi were still men of tremendous power at the time of Christ, but they were foreigners as far as the Roman Empire was concerned. Rome was fearful of eastern influences. Nearly every previous world empire, including the Assyrian, Babylonian, Medo-Persian, and Greek empires, had been oriented toward the east. Those empires had all expanded eastward, because territories in the east were more accessible to their land-based armies. Alexander the Great, for example, conquered as far east as the Indus river. His death in 323 B.C. began the decline of Greece as a world power, and the next great empire was Rome.

The territory conquered by Rome, on the other hand, looked westward and northward. Rome virtually enveloped the Mediterranean Sea and covered most of what is now Europe. While Rome was busy conquering those lands, a rival empire, the Parthian Empire, was spreading from the east through Mesopotamia, right up to the eastern boundaries of Rome. Parthia covered much of the same territory ruled by the Medes and the Persians and the old Babylonian Empire. Rome never successfully conquered the Parthians, whom they viewed as a great threat to their eastern borders.

The descendants of the original magi still held great power in Parthia. Like their predecessors in the Babylonian, Medo-Persian, and Grecian empires, these magi served as key advisors to the king. In fact, the magi were partly responsible for choosing the kings of Parthia.

Magi in the Court of Herod

When magi from the east arrived in Jerusalem, Herod was understandably troubled. He knew these men were king-makers, and they were going about town asking for the One who had been born King of the Jews! Try to imagine the scene. These men arrived in Jerusalem no doubt with a great deal of pomp and show. Their typical costume would have included long, cone-shaped hats like those we associate with wizards. They would have been riding not on camels, but more likely on Persian steeds or Arabian horses. They might well have been traveling with a small army, since their journey took them into Roman territory. They must have been an imposing sight!

Furthermore, Herod's own small army was on duty with the census. This was no time for a band of foreign king-

How Did Santa Claus Originate?

The model for Santa Claus was a fourth-century Christian bishop named Saint Nicholas. Little is known about the real Nicholas, except that he was probably the bishop of Lycia. In the Middle Ages, when it became popular to venerate saints, legends about Nicholas began to flourish. One said he had given three bags of gold to the daughters of a poor man so that the girls would not have to earn their dowries through prostitution. Another claimed he had miraculously restored three little boys to life after they had been cut up for bacon. Thus Nicholas became known as a giver of gifts and the patron saint of children. His day is December 6.

Nicholas was particularly popular in Holland. It is there that the customs linking Nicholas to Christmas seem to have first begun. Dutch children expected the friendly saint to visit them during the night on December 5, and they developed the custom of placing their wooden shoes by the fireplace to be filled with gifts. Santa Claus is the Americanization of his Dutch name, *Sinterklaas*.

Of course, by the time Santa Claus became a part of American lore, children had discovered that you can get a lot more gifts in a sock than you can in a wooden shoe, so that adjustment to the custom was made in the mid-nineteenth century.

Clement Moore, an American poet, may be more responsible than any other person for popularizing the myth of Santa Claus. He wrote "A Visit from St. Nicholas" in 1822 which begins with the famous line, "'Twas the night before Christmas," and it was published in the Troy New York *Sentinel*. It was immediately popular and has endured ever since.

makers to be inquiring about an infant they called "King of the Jews." That was, after all, Herod's title, given to him by Caesar Augustus himself, at Herod's coronation.

Herod was in a difficult spot geographically as well. His region formed a very small buffer between Rome and Parthia. It had already been a battleground in several wars between the two world powers. He undoubtedly saw the magi as a serious threat to the stability of his kingdom. When Matthew 2:3 says "he was troubled," it uses a word that means "shaken," or "agitated"—like the heavy-duty cycle of a washing machine: In other words, he was in great turmoil.

Apparently, though, Herod wisely decided to take the diplomatic approach. Matthew tells us he called all the Jewish experts in and asked them where the Christ was to be born. Then he summoned the magi and told them, "Go and make careful search for the Child; and when you have found Him, report to me, that I too may come and worship Him" (v. 8).

For their part, the magi must have assumed that everyone in Israel would know about the new King's birth and could tell them where He was. Imagine their surprise when they began asking people in Jerusalem, "Where is He who has been born King of the Jews?" (v. 2), and no one seemed to know what they were talking about!

We don't know how they knew the Messianic prophecies had been fulfilled, but obviously God revealed it to them in some way. He confirmed it with the sign of a star. Perhaps they drew the connection between that star and Numbers 24:17: "A star shall come forth from Jacob, and a scepter shall rise from Israel, and shall crush through the forehead of Moab, and tear down all the sons of Sheth." Being astrologers, if they had ever read that verse, they would have been keenly interested in it. Of all the verses in the Old Testament, they would have been drawn to that one—it is the only one

that talks about a star being any kind of sign. And "a scepter
. . . from Israel" *does* seem to suggest a King of the Jews.
Perhaps they had figured that out. We are not told.

Every Christmas the planetariums and astronomers
offer explanations of the Christmas star. Some say it must
have been Jupiter, or a comet, or the conjunction of two
planets, or some other natural phenomenon. None of those
explanations is plausible, because the star led them right to
the house where Jesus was. No known natural occurrence
could have done that.

What was the star? No one knows, and Scripture doesn't
say, but the biblical phenomenon that most closely resembles
it is the shekinah glory, the visual expression of God's glory,
which in the time of Moses led Israel to the Promised Land,
appearing as a pillar of cloud by day and a pillar of fire by
night (Exodus 13:21). It was the same glory that shone on the
shepherds when they learned of Christ's birth (Luke 2:9).
Perhaps what the magi saw was a similar manifestation of
God's glory, which appeared to them like a star.

Whatever the star was, it signified to them that Jesus
had been born. After they left Herod, it reappeared and
"went on before them, until it came and stood over where the
Child was" (Matthew 2:9).

Magi in the Presence of Jesus

The place where they found Jesus was not, by the way,
the stable where Jesus was born. Verse 11 says they found
Him in a house. This may have occurred months—even as
much as two years—after Jesus' birth. Matthew says Herod
ascertained from the magi when the star appeared (v. 7).
Then when he learned they were not going to reveal Jesus'
location to him, Herod "became very enraged, and sent and
slew all the male children who were in Bethlehem and in all

its environs, from *two years old* and under, according to the time which he had ascertained from the magi" (v. 16, emphasis added). Of course, it could be that Herod just wanted to be doubly certain he had exterminated the newborn King, so he killed every child under two in the area. But this could also be an indication that these events occurred that long after the birth of Christ.

Either way, the wise men found Jesus in a house, not in a stable. "They came into the house and saw the Child with Mary His mother; and they fell down and worshiped Him; and opening their treasures they presented to Him gifts of gold and frankincense and myrrh" (v. 11). God in His grace had led these men out of a pagan land, and they found themselves face to face with the Savior.

It is significant that they worshiped. They may have actually begun seeking Him because of political motivations. Perhaps they thought this new King would help the Parthians defeat Rome. Maybe they were even looking for a new king to unify the two empires. Possibly they were simply curious about the long-prophesied Jewish Messiah. Or it could be that they were genuinely seeking the true God. Whatever their motives at the start of their journey, when they saw Him, "they fell down and worshiped Him" (v. 11). God in His grace opened their eyes to something His own people did not see—that Jesus was God in human form.

I take it from their response that they were converted and thus became the earliest Gentile believers in Christ. That makes an ironic beginning to Matthew's gospel. Writing specifically to Jewish readers, he begins with this account of a group of Gentile mystics who recognized the King of the Jews—and he finishes by showing how His own people rejected and killed their King. The apostle John wrote in a similar vein: "He came to His own, and those who were His own did not receive Him. But as many as received Him, to them He gave the right to become children of God, even to those who believe in His name" (John 1:11–12).

The gifts of the magi had special significance. Gold and frankincense would be typical gifts for a king. Gold, the most precious metal then known to man, was a common symbol of royalty from the earliest times and remains so today. Frankincense, an expensive fragrance, had special significance in Old Testament worship (Leviticus 2:2). It was often sprinkled on offerings in the Temple. The frankincense may therefore have had additional meaning in signifying Jesus' deity.

Myrrh, on the other hand, was a curious gift for a newborn king. It was a substance used in embalming the dead (John 19:39). Mixed with wine, it had an anesthetic effect. When Jesus was crucified, He was offered a myrrh and wine mixture, but He refused it (Mark 15:23).

The gift of myrrh therefore seems to foreshadow Jesus' suffering and death. There's no indication that the magi foresaw the details of this. But it is likely that just as God had led the magi to the infant Jesus, He had also guided them in the selection of their gifts, so that the combination of gifts they brought would testify to the new King's royalty, His deity, and His death on behalf of humanity.

Whether they realized it or not, the child they were kneeling before would one day grow up to suffer and die for their sakes. His death would pay the price of their sins. Because of that coming sacrifice, the magi, whose lives had been spent in sorcery, wizardry, and the occult, could be forgiven and transformed by His power.

Scripture is silent about what became of the magi after their visit. I am confident that God, who revealed Jesus' birth to them, led them to where He was, and warned them about Herod in a dream, also saw to it that they had enough truth to be brought to full spiritual maturity in Christ.

Matthew tells us that the magi, "having been warned by God in a dream not to return to Herod . . . departed for their own country by another way" (Matthew 2:12). There almost seems to be a double meaning in that statement. They returned to their country by a different geographical route, to be sure. But they also were now followers of another way in the spiritual sense. That's true of everyone who turns to Christ and becomes one of His worshipers in spirit and truth: "If any man is in Christ, he is a new creature; the old things passed away; behold, new things have come" (2 Corinthians 5:17).

"Wise men still seek Him," the familiar slogan says. It's true. In all the world, there are only two kinds of people: those who are fools and those who are wise. Herod typifies one brand of fool, who overtly rejects the Savior. The Jewish religious leaders who counseled Herod were fools of a different kind. They didn't hate Jesus; they just didn't care about Him. They ignored Him. They were too busy and too wrapped up in themselves to bother with Him—just like most people today.

The magi, on the other hand, were true wise men. It wasn't convenient for them to come to Jesus, but they realized they had no option. Although it meant great sacrifice for them, they doggedly pursued until they found Him. They typify every true wise man—or woman—who has ever lived.

How about you? Who or what takes first place in your life? That is the only measure of whether you are a fool or wise. You fit in one category or the other, for your only possible responses to Christ are to hate Him, neglect Him, or like the magi, adore Him.

In Christ "are hidden all the treasures of wisdom and knowledge" (Colossians 2:3). May you be truly wise.

Born to Die

On that very first Christmas, earth was oblivious to all that was happening. But heaven wasn't. The holy angels were waiting in anticipation to break forth in praise and worship and adoration at the birth of the newborn Child. This Child's birth meant deliverance for mankind. The angel told Joseph: "It is He who will save His people from their sins" (Matthew 1:21). Jesus knew that to do that, He would have to die.

I envision a farewell that I think must have taken place in heaven on the first Christmas Eve. I imagine the Son might have said good-bye to the Father and the Father to the Son. In fact, I'm sure it happened, because the Son's good-bye message is recorded in Hebrews 10:5–7: "When He comes into the world, He says, 'Sacrifice and offering Thou hast not desired, but a body Thou hast prepared for Me; in whole burnt offerings and sacrifices for sin Thou hast taken no pleasure.' Then I said, 'Behold, I have come . . . to do Thy will, O God.'"

That passage of Scripture gives us a remarkable look at the heart of the Savior before His birth. He knew He was entering the world to be the final and ultimate sacrifice for sin. His body had been divinely prepared by God specifically for that purpose. Jesus was going to die for the sins of the world, and He knew it. Moreover, He was doing it willingly. That was the whole point of the incarnation.

The important issue of Christmas is not so much that Jesus came, but *why* He came. There was no salvation in His birth. Nor did the sinless way He lived His life have any redemptive force of its own. His example, as flawless as it was, could not rescue men from their sins. Even His teaching, the greatest truth ever revealed to man, could not save us from our sins. There was a price to be paid for our sins. Someone had to die. Only Jesus could do it.

Jesus came to earth, of course, to reveal God to mankind. He came to teach truth. He came to fulfill the Law. He came to offer His kingdom. He came to show us how to live. He came to reveal God's love. He came to bring peace. He came to heal the sick. He came to minister to the needy.

But all those reasons are incidental to His ultimate purpose. He could have done them all without being born as a human. He could have simply appeared—like the angel of the Lord often did in the Old Testament—and accomplished everything in the above list, without literally becoming a man. But He had one more reason for coming: He came to die.

Here's a side to the Christmas story that isn't often told: those soft little hands, fashioned by the Holy Spirit in Mary's womb, were made so that nails might be driven through them. Those baby feet, pink and unable to walk, would one day walk up a dusty hill to be nailed to a cross. That sweet infant's head with sparkling eyes and eager mouth was formed so that someday men might force a crown of thorns onto it. That tender body, warm and soft, wrapped in swaddling clothes, would one day be ripped open by a spear.

Jesus was born to die.

Don't think I'm trying to put a damper on your Christmas spirit. Far from it—for Jesus' death, though devised and carried out by men with evil intentions, was in no sense a tragedy. In fact, it represents the greatest victory over

evil anyone has ever accomplished. There are several reasons for that, all summed up in Hebrews 2:9–18. We'll look at selected verses from this passage as we go along.

He Became a Substitute for Us

Jesus' death was no tragedy, first of all, because He died as our substitute: "We do see Him who has been made for a little while lower than the angels, namely, Jesus, because of the suffering of death crowned with glory and honor, that by the grace of God He might taste death for everyone" (v. 9).

He was the One who created the angels. But in His incarnation, our Lord made Himself lower than them. This does not mean, of course, that He became less than God or that He gave up any aspect of His deity. "For a little while," however, He stepped down to a level that was lower than the angels. In what sense was He lower than the angels? "Because of the suffering of death crowned with glory and honor" (v. 9). No angel could ever die. Death is reserved for mortals, and Jesus had to die.

For what reason? "That by the grace of God He might taste death for everyone" (v. 9). He was our substitute. When He was nailed on the cross He died for you and He died for me. He died for everyone.

Notice the phrase "the suffering of death" in verse 9. Think for a moment about how Jesus died. It was not an easy, gentle passing from this world. It was excruciating agony and torture of the worst kind, for it was on a cross. He *suffered* in His death. He drank the bitter cup at Calvary in its fullness—He drained it to the last drop. He experienced all the pain, all the loneliness, all the torments that have ever been associated with death. Yet He did it voluntarily, so that He might receive what we deserve, so that we don't have to. That's what Scripture means when it says, "Christ died for our sins" (1 Corinthians 15:3).

The death He tasted was the penalty of our sin. He received the full force of all that the devil could throw at Him. More than that, He received the full expression of God's wrath over sin. In a few hours on that cross, Jesus absorbed the full penalty of sin. If we were to suffer hell for all eternity, we would never pay the full price. But He gathered up an eternity of punishment, paid it all, and walked away from it a risen Savior. *That* is power! In every possible dimension, Jesus Christ took all the pain and agony of death and tasted every bit of it—for us.

Death was not God's plan for mankind in the beginning; it is part of the curse of sin. God had warned Adam that if he disobeyed and ate of the forbidden fruit, he would die (Genesis 2:17). Adam disobeyed, and introduced sin and death to the human race (Romans 5:12), where it has been passed down to everyone who has ever been born—except One. Ezekiel wrote, "The soul who sins will die" (Ezekiel 18:4). Paul wrote, "The wages of sin is death" (Romans 6:23). Sin inevitably brings death, and there is no reason for death except sin.

As we have seen, Jesus was conceived and born without a human father—and therefore without sin. He was guilty of nothing. He never sinned. He could have escaped death for Himself, but He chose to die as a substitute for us, bearing our sin. The sinless One took the sin of the entire world. The One who is life itself died. The perfect One became the punished one. He paid the price of our sin and made our redemption possible.

A student at The Master's College was struggling to pay his fees. A financial crisis in his family left him unable to meet his obligations. He had all but resigned himself to the reality that he would have to leave school. On the day before his payment came due, an anonymous donor paid the bill in full. When the student came in to withdraw from school, he learned his bill had been paid by someone else. He had no further obligation. He was able to continue his education.

In a sense, that's what Jesus did for us. We incurred a great debt—too great for us to pay. He paid the debt. Thus He freed us from the obligation of God's justice, which is death for sin, and He liberated us to experience God's grace and love. It's as simple as that.

That's what we call the grace of God. He didn't come because we asked for or deserved His intervention, but because He is a God of grace. His lovingkindness toward us is absolutely undeserved. Christ chose to die for us solely on the basis of His sovereign good will.

Do you realize that no one in the universe could have taken Jesus' life if He had not given it up willingly? Jesus said, "For this reason the Father loves Me, because I lay down My life that I may take it again. No one has taken it away from Me, but I lay it down on My own initiative. I have authority to lay it down, and I have authority to take it up again" (John 10:17–18). Jesus voluntarily gave His life; no one took it from Him. His love was overwhelming. He looked at sinful man, He saw the inevitability of death and hell, and He paid the price Himself. Nothing deterred Him from that. Even when He came to earth and the mass of people rejected Him, mocked Him, hated Him, and even killed Him, that didn't stifle His grace. As He died, He prayed, "Father, forgive them; for they do not know what they are doing" (Luke 23:34).

He Pioneered Our Salvation

A second reason Jesus' death was no tragedy is that His death was what made it possible for Him to pioneer our salvation. Verse 10 of Hebrews 2 says, "It was fitting for Him, for whom are all things, and through whom are all things, in bringing many sons to glory, to perfect the author of their salvation through sufferings." Now at first sight, that verse may seem a little difficult, but we want to focus mainly on the phrase that refers to Christ as "the author of . . . salvation." That will clarify the meaning of the entire verse.

The word translated "author" means "pioneer," "leader," or "trailblazer." You get the idea. It refers to someone who starts something for others to follow. The word could refer to the founder of a city, or to the leader of a pioneer exploration. It cannot refer to someone who stands at the rear and issues orders. And it cannot refer to someone who follows a path that has already been laid out.

So what does this verse mean by calling Christ the author of salvation? It means He is the pacesetter, the pioneer, the one who leads the way. He is the first and only initiator of salvation. There is no way to get to God apart from Him. Jesus said, "I am the way, and the truth, and the life; no one comes to the Father, but through Me" (John 14:6). Scripture is clear; there is only one path to God, and Jesus is the trailblazer: "There is salvation in no one else; for there is no other name under heaven that has been given among men, by which we must be saved" (Acts 4:12).

The same word is used in Hebrews 5:8–9: "Although He was a Son, He learned obedience from the things which He suffered. And having been made perfect, He became to all those who obey Him the source [author] of eternal salvation." Again, that verse highlights His suffering. The suffering was essential to salvation. Jesus could not bring people to God with unpunished sin. So He paid the price, and His sufferings made Him the perfect leader. His death opened the path—blazed the trail wide—so that He could bring "many sons to glory."

He Sanctified His People

A third great victory was accomplished in Jesus' death: "Both He who sanctifies and those who are sanctified are all from one Father; for which reason He is not ashamed to call them brethren, saying, 'I will proclaim Thy name to My brethren, In the midst of the congregation I will sing Thy praise.' And again, 'I will put My trust in Him.' And again, 'Behold, I and the children whom God has given Me'" (Hebrews 2:11–13).

"Sanctify" means "set apart," or "make holy." This passage is saying that Jesus Christ is holy, and that He is capable of making us holy.

Perhaps the greatest theological dilemma of all time was resolved at the cross. It was the question of how a holy God could communicate mercy and grace to sinful people. Sin, as we have seen, demands death. Yet God's lovingkindness and mercy are never-ending. He loves sinners. If he simply accepted us as we are and ignored our sin, His own holiness would be tainted. Christ resolved the question by taking our punishment on Himself. He brought mercy and justice together at the cross—and satisfied the demands of both.

How many of our sins did He pay for? All of them. Just the ones in the past, or the future ones, too? All of them. Thus He can righteously deal with us as if we were sinless. He has declared us holy. Positionally, we are as holy and spotless as sinless creatures (Ephesians 1:4; 5:27; Colossians 1:22).

Of course, we are not sinless in practice, but part of Christ's sanctifying work is the transformation of our desires and actions (2 Corinthians 5:17; Galatians 5:24; Titus 2:12). He is conforming us to His image, sanctifying even our behavior (Romans 8:29; 2 Corinthians 3:18; Ephesians 4:24). He's making us more and more like Himself.

The holiness with which He sanctifies us cannot be marred. "For by one offering He has perfected for all time those who are sanctified" (Hebrews 10:14). Once you have received the imputed holiness of Jesus Christ, nothing in this universe can take it away. Christ paid the penalty for sin in full, and your sins can never again be brought up against you. "Who will bring a charge against God's elect? God is the one who justifies; who is the one who condemns? Christ Jesus is He who died, yes, rather who was raised, who is at the right hand of God, who also intercedes for us" (Romans 8:33–34). No one—not even the accuser, Satan—can recall our sins to use them against us.

Don't miss this remarkable statement: "He is not ashamed to call them brethren" (Hebrews 2:11). Most of us would have to admit that we have been ashamed of Jesus Christ more times than we would like to admit. Why should we be? There is nothing about Him that we need to be ashamed of. He is not ashamed of us, although lots of things about us might legitimately make Him ashamed. We sin. We disappoint Him. We disobey Him.

Yet He sanctifies us. Positionally, we are perfectly holy, like Him. And so He calls us brothers.

There is no hierarchy among brothers. This verse is saying we are one with Christ. We share the same holiness. We are as acceptable to God as if we were as sinless as Christ. We are part of the same family. We have the same Father. We are brothers. Christ calls us brothers without shame.

The Christ of God—the holy, sinless One whom angels adored—became lower than the angels to suffer and die to be our substitute, to pioneer the way to heaven, and to sanctify us. He even stoops to call us brothers and sisters, fellow-heirs. And He does it without shame. Can you resist that kind of love? I can't.

He Conquered Satan

Here's another reason Jesus' death was no tragedy: "Since . . . the children share in flesh and blood, He Himself likewise also partook of the same, that through death He

might render powerless him who had the power of death, that is, the devil" (Hebrews 2:14).

Did you realize that one of the main reasons for the incarnation was so Christ could deliver a death blow to Satan? As we have seen, the first prophecy ever given about Jesus predicted that He would crush the serpent's head (Genesis 3:15). Here, in the New Testament, is the proclamation that the ancient prophecy was fulfilled.

Satan's great power is death. He is the paymaster for the wages of sin. If he can keep a person living in sin until death, he's got that person forever.

Someone had to conquer death to destroy Satan's weapon, and that's exactly what Jesus did. He came out of the grave, exploded out of the shackles of death, and announced, "Because I live, you shall live also" (John 14:19). And so we say, "O death, where is your victory? O death, where is your sting?" (1 Corinthians 15:55).

He Became Our High Priest

Finally, Christ's death was a great triumph because He became our sympathetic high priest: "Therefore, He had to be made like His brethren in all things, that He might become a merciful and faithful high priest in things pertaining to God, to make propitiation for the sins of the people. For since He Himself was tempted in that which He has suffered, He is able to come to the aid of those who are tempted" (Hebrews 2:17–18).

That is one of the most remarkable passages in all of Scripture. What can it possibly mean? That He learned something in His incarnation He did not know before? No. There has never been anything He did not know. It was not a question of His gaining some knowledge or experience He needed.

But to be a sympathetic high priest, He had to be a man.

A high priest is a mediator between men and God. Obviously, a high priest would have to understand to some degree the mind of God and also the mind of man. And the perfect high priest would be someone who was in fact both God and man. That's exactly who Jesus Christ is—the perfect mediator.

These verses bring to mind the parallel ideas expressed in Hebrews 4:15: "We do not have a high priest who cannot sympathize with our weaknesses, but One who has been tempted in all things as we are, yet without sin." He was made like us in all things—even to the point of experiencing the same temptations. The only difference is that He was without sin.

He was hungry. He was thirsty. He was overcome with fatigue. He slept. He grew. He loved. He was astonished. He marveled. He was glad. He grieved. He became angry. He was troubled. He read the Scripture. He prayed all night. He wept. He is one of us in every sense—the perfect sympathizer.

And He is God—the perfect high priest.

Take another look at the manger this Christmas. Look beyond the tender scene, and see what Jesus Himself knew even before He came—that He was born to die.

He died for you. He bore your sin. He purchased your salvation. He guaranteed your sanctification. He destroyed your enemy. And He became a sympathetic high priest. Even as you read this, He is seated next to the Father in heaven, ready to make intercession for you (Hebrews 7:25).

> Let all mortal flesh keep silence,
> And with fear and trembling stand
> Ponder nothing earthly minded,
> For with blessing in His hand,
> Christ our God to earth descendeth,
> Our full homage to demand.

King of Kings, yet born of Mary,
As of old on earth He stood,
Lord of lords, in human vesture,
In the body and the blood,
He will give to all the faithful
His own self for heavenly food.*

---

*From the fifth-century *Liturgy of St. James.* Adapted by Gerald Moultrie, 1864.

Christmas Presents

Christmas is a good time for giving. After all, we are celebrating the greatest gift ever given—God's Son: "For God so loved the world, that He gave His only begotten Son, that whoever believes in Him should not perish, but have eternal life" (John 3:16).

God's great Gift was first of all a gift of love to an unworthy world. He gave not because He had to, but because He loves us. And our giving should reflect His love. If we can keep that perspective—especially in the minds of our children—this can be one of the most blessed and enjoyable aspects of the holiday.

It isn't easy to keep one's perspective so focused. Christmas has become too commercial, too carefully merchandised, too crassly materialistic to lend itself to teaching *any* spiritual truth about giving. Every year at Christmas, the buying frenzy gets worse. Have you ever noticed, for example, how much stuff is sold that nobody needs? It doesn't have any practical use. It just sits there, collecting dust.

Our society is literally filled with the unnecessary, the insignificant, and the meaningless. And people spend a fortune on that kind of junk for Christmas. Why? Often, it is the quickest and easiest way to complete an obligatory Christmas list. What meaning is there in that?

Ask yourself this year if your giving reflects the spirit of Him who gave His best for us—just because He loves us.

O Come Let Us Adore Him

What is the right response to Christmas? What should characterize the way we observe the holiday? An emphasis on peace toward men? The spirit of giving? Joy and gladness? Kindness to our fellow man? All those things are good, but they are inadequate responses to the birth of Christ—unless they are the products of a worshipful heart.

When I was in high school, a friend and I went to a party. We didn't know what kind of party it was going to be, but my friend liked a girl who he knew would be there. I agreed to go with him. When we got to the party, it was very dark and slow music was playing. Some couples were dancing, and some were in the corners, but everyone seemed to be locked in embraces. It wasn't hard to see what direction the party was going. Neither I nor my friend really wanted to be at that kind of party. I suggested we leave. He had a better idea. "Do you want to change the complexion of this party?" he asked, with a twinkle in his eye.

I have to admit that I took a sort of perverse glee in what we did. We found the fuse box and flipped the switch that controlled the record player. Of course, everyone was upset, but they didn't know what had happened. My friend and I came in just then with an armload of games and led everyone into the living room. For the rest of that evening,

everyone had a great time playing games. It turned out to be a terrific party.

I've often thought I want to do the same kind of thing to Christmas. I would like very much to pull the plug on the world's party, because I'm convinced there's an even better way to celebrate Christmas—one that's full of true joy and gladness, not the silly frivolity and careless gaiety most people settle for.

It begins, of course, with realizing the true significance of Jesus' birth. That means we must see beyond the familiar elements of Christmas and realize that at its heart Christmas is a celebration of the incarnation of God. If you see what Christmas really means, your immediate response will be worship.

Worship is the missing element in the monstrosity that Christmas has become. I'm not suggesting that there is anything wrong with putting up decorations, spending time with our families, getting together with friends, exchanging gifts, or many of the other things we do to celebrate the holiday. Those things add to the joy of the season, and they're all legitimate. But apart from worship, they are utterly inadequate responses to the reality of the Savior's birth. The first priority in all our celebrating should be worship, and everything else we do should flow out of adoring hearts.

When I speak of worship, by the way, I'm not referring to religious activity. I'm not talking about something that must happen in church, or before an altar, or kneeling in a closet. I don't mean performing a ritual, saying a memorized prayer, or any of the things most people tend to associate with worship. Worship is more than activity. It is first a state of the heart.

Worship can be expressed in many ways. Several years ago, I did a study on worship. Out of that study I wrote a book, in which I concluded that one of God's chief aims in saving sinners is to make them true worshipers.* What amazed me in studying the theme of worship in the Bible was realizing that true worship can be expressed in countless ways. We tend to think of worship as either ritualized ceremony, singing, praying, or sitting quietly and reflecting—in short, the kind of thing we usually do in church.

Actually, though, when the Bible speaks of worship, it almost never means something that takes place in a communal religious service. Worship as Scripture portrays it is always intensely practical, involving sacrifice (Romans 12:1–2), giving (Philippians 4:18), service to others (Hebrews 13:16), proclaiming the good news of salvation (Romans 15:16), and otherwise living one's life as a testimony of God's truth. A heart of praise and adoration weaves all such activity into the fabric of worship.

In saying Christmas should be a time of worship, I'm not suggesting that we eliminate everything but formal worship from our Christmas traditions. Rather, I'm saying we need to start all over. We need to begin with worship, and let our worship rule how we celebrate the holiday. I'm calling for the radical approach—the fuse-box solution.

To put it in practical terms, I'm saying we should worship like the shepherds did. They dropped everything they were doing to attend His birth. There is a sense of urgency and godly determination in the way they came to Him: "It came about that when the angels had gone away from them into heaven, the shepherds began saying to one another, 'Let us go *straight to Bethlehem* then, and see this thing that has happened which the Lord has made known to us.' *And they came in haste* and found their way to Mary and Joseph, and the Baby as He lay in the manger" (Luke 2:15–16, emphasis added).

The Ultimate Priority (Chicago: Moody, 1983).

That isn't all. They also shared the news with everyone around: "When they had seen this, they made known the statement which had been told them about this Child" (v. 17). Christmas is a wonderful opportunity to speak to others about the Savior. That's one way we can express our adoration of Christ.

We can also worship as the magi did. "They fell down and worshiped Him; and opening their treasures they presented to Him gifts of gold and frankincense and myrrh" (Matthew 2:11). They brought Him gifts. We give gifts to others at Christmas. Have you ever thought of giving Christ a gift on His birthday? It is one more way you can worship.

Mary worshiped through quiet reflection. She "treasured up all these things, pondering them in her heart" (Luke 2:19). In the busyness and chaos of the holiday season, have you ever taken time to meditate on Christ? That is another practical way you can worship Him.

The apostle Paul wrote, "Thanks be to God for His indescribable gift!" (2 Corinthians 9:15). That should be our response to Christmas. If your heart is not overwhelmed with gratitude and adoration, then you're missing the whole point of Christmas.

God has given the greatest Christmas gift of all time: "For God so loved the world, that He gave His only begotten Son, that whoever believes in Him should not perish, but have eternal life" (John 3:16).

And Christ gave His all for us: "Although He existed in the form of God, He did not regard equality with God a thing to be grasped, but emptied Himself, taking the form of a bond-servant, and being made in the likeness of men" (Philippians 2:6–7).

How else can we respond, but by giving ourselves to Him completely in return?

Next Time It Will Be Different!

The First Time Jesus Came:

He came veiled in the form of a child.
A star marked His arrival.
Wise men brought Him gifts.
There was no room for Him.
Only a few attended His arrival.
He came as a baby.

The Next Time Jesus Comes:

He will be recognized by all.
Heaven will be lit by His glory.
He will bring rewards for His own.
The world won't be able to contain
    His glory.
Every eye shall see Him.
He will come as Sovereign King and
    Lord of all.

TOPICAL INDEX

137

SCRIPTURE INDEX